TRADITIONAL WEAVERS *of* GUATEMALA

Their Stories, Their Lives

DEBORAH CHANDLER AND TERESA CORDÓN

PHOTOGRAPHY BY JOE COCA

OTHER BOOKS BY DEBORAH CHANDLER

Learning to Weave. Interweave Press, 1984

Guatemalan Woven Wealth: Preserving a Rich Textile Tradition.
With Raymond Senuk. Friendship Bridge, 2009

Editor: Linda Ligon
Copy editor: Veronica Patterson
Design and illustration: Michael Angelo Signorella

Text ©2015 Deborah Chandler and Teresa Cordón
Photography ©2015 Joe Coca

Cover image: Ana Ceto, a backstrap weaver of Santa María Nebaj, Guatemala

THRUMS LLC

306 North Washington Avenue
Loveland, Colorado 80537
USA

Printed in China by Asia Pacific
Library of Congress Control Number 2015934892

· DEDICATIONS ·

To my mother, who taught me how to see, and
to my father, who taught me how to put words to what I saw.
Deborah

To my mother, who loved to have people read to her, and
to my sisters who did it. To my father, who always had a book in his pocket.
Teresa

· PREFACE ·

Our publisher, Linda Ligon, has been to Guatemala many times, soaking up all the Maya color and culture she could on every trip. So when she proposed that it was time for us to work together on a book showcasing weavers such as she was doing in Peru and Mexico, how could the answer be anything but yes?

If I were reading this book one of my big questions would be, "With more than half a million weavers to choose from, why these twenty? What makes them so special, the chosen few?"

The range of textile techniques used in Guatemala is quietly amazing. To the non-textile person it's nearly all about color, an abundance that is as visceral as it is visual. To a textile craftsperson, looking more closely reveals more than a dozen kinds of looms, more than a dozen ways to do brocade, more than a dozen non-loom techniques, and dozens of yarns and other materials that are both expected and totally surprising. In short, more variety than anyone would guess on first glance. We wanted to include as much of that variety as possible. The western and northern highlands region of Guatemala is made up of eleven departments (states) and we also wanted to include artisans from as many as we could, each area having specialties. (We managed nine, in which seven languages are spoken.) There were other factors we took into account as well, many of which expanded from our initial vision. Elders, we found out, become so in their fifties. How closely did we want to define "weaver"? And so on.

In our search we spoke with everyone we know who works with fiber artisans of any kind. We told them who we were looking for and through word of mouth and many avenues we found this mix of people. There was no list. We found each artisan down a different path.

For these artisans, life is not remembered in linear form, with a clock and a calendar in hand. Life is stories, family events, community activity, births and deaths and everything in between. As we say later in this book, these are the stories of the artisans as they remember them and told them to us. As we listened there were the issues of language, of cultural context, of trust, of our knowledge or understanding of the subject at hand…. All of these and more shaped what grew into a rich body of information.

When a thought or statement is translated through three languages, Kaqchikel to Spanish to English for instance, the words change, the punctuation changes, original nuance may be lost. Likewise, given the many factors involved, the telling of family history is sure to be altered somewhat. In the end, we believe that we have delivered the spirit of the artisans and their stories, if not the precise grammatical structure of their lives.

Throughout this book you will likely encounter unfamiliar words, in multiple languages. There is a glossary at the back that will help. In order to make it a little easier from the start, here we want to define some of the words that you will see often so you can slide right by them.

Warp—the threads that are attached to the loom and run lengthwise in finished cloth

Weft—the cross threads woven into the warp, the horizontal threads in finished cloth

Brocade—patterns woven with an extra weft, often in a contrasting color, and often a heavier weight of yarn. It is so common in backstrap-woven fabrics that we often don't use the term: it is a given.

Huipil—a Maya woman's traditional upper garment, heavier than a blouse and usually with less shaping.

Maya vs. Mayan—When to use which is debated by many. We defer to current scholarly conventions.

As for that great variety of looms, techniques, and materials, in addition to what we learned from the artisans themselves we wanted some historical perspective. Nearly everyone talked of changes in style in their lifetimes; is that new or has it always been going on? Looms may not have changed in a hundred years but materials certainly have. The books and websites we studied to deepen our understanding are also listed in the back of this book. Finally you will find a list of museums and organizations actively working to support textile artisans.

In everything here—artisans, textiles, vocabulary, references, organizations—we have shown you only the tip of the iceberg. An entire lifetime could be spent learning about Guatemalan textiles and the women and men who make them. And still there would be more.

· ACKNOWLEDGMENTS ·

First we want to thank the people who helped us to know the artisans: Gloria Chonay, Manuel Morales and Mirna Aguilar, Jody Slocum, David Glanville, Salvador Ajtzip Sosóf, Diego Mendoza, Ilana Schatz and David Lindgren, Clemente Ruiz, Teodoro Xiloj, Manuel Lux and María Raymundo, Teresa Gomez, Tomás Pérez, Limitless Horizons Ixil, Ana Eymi Canay Canay, Edilma Hernandez de Raymundo, Olga Reiche, Carlos Tista, Gilberta Gonzales, Brenda Rosenbaum, Julio Cardona, and Marta Cordón.

Thanks to Pueblo to People, which gave Teresa the opportunity to expand her connections with artisans and through which Teresa and Deborah met in the first place, and to Mayan Hands for the wealth of experience working with Mayan women artisans it gave to Deborah.

As always, an immeasurable thanks to Linda Ligon, editor, publisher, and friend, whose impetus and guidance make all the difference.

And finally, of course, a profound and humble thanks to the women and men who shared their stories for the benefit of all of us. Dios les bendiga.

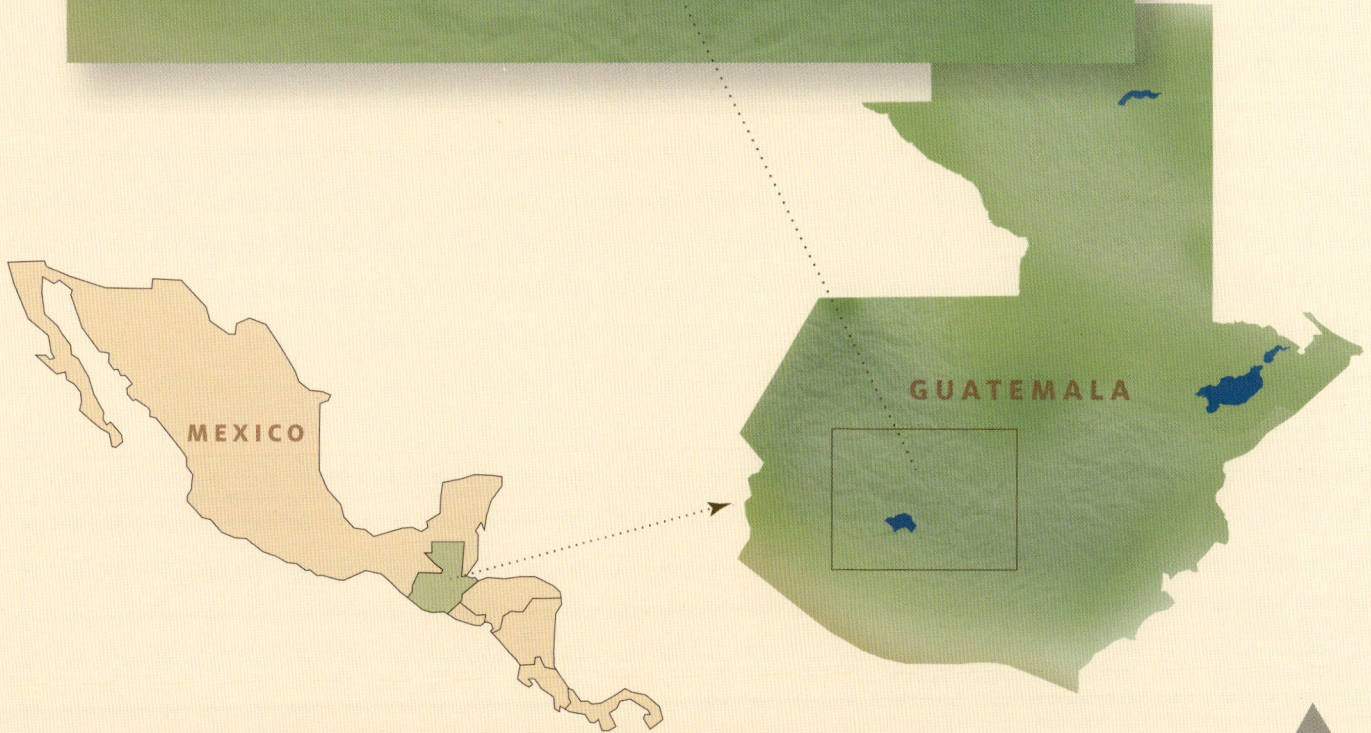

San Gaspar Chajul

Santa Maria Nebaj

San Juan Cotzal

Samac

Cobán

Tactic

Santa Lucia la Reforma

Momostenango

Rabinal

Salcajá

San José Poaquil

Zunil

Santa Apolonia

Santigo Atitlán

Guatemala City

San Antonio Aguas Calientes

MEXICO

GUATEMALA

NORTH

THE FOUNDING OF IXIMCHE:

Arbol de Maiz—Tree of Corn
and Tecpan Quauhtemallan—Royal City
with Wood Fortification Surrounded
by Ample Forests

With more than two dozen distinct ethnic groups within the territory now known as Guatemala, over the centuries alliances and opponents have ebbed and flowed. In the 1400s, the two largest groups, the K'iche's and the Kaqchikels, were living side by side in a comfortable alliance. The K'iche' capital was Utatlan, a short distance from present-day Santa Cruz del Quiché. (Quiché is the geographic name; K'iche' is the name of the language and the people. Both are pronounced key CHAY.) The Kaqchikel base was in Chiavar, the site of present day Chichicastenango, Quiché.

In 1425, the K'iche' leader Quicab came to power. According to one version, the conflicts that began during his reign came from within his own family, and his affection for the Kaqchikels continued. According to another version, there were Kaqchikels involved in the growing unrest. Either way, it became evident that the Kaqchikels would be well-advised to move.

They chose a new site and began building, and by 1470, they were able to move into Iximche, Tree of Corn, in an area called Tecpan Quauhtemallan, meaning "Royal City with Wood Fortification Surrounded by Ample Forests." The timing was good. In 1475, Quicab died, and by 1476, the K'iche'/Kaqchikel war had begun in earnest.

Now, more than five hundred years later, there are three points of pride embedded in Iximche. First is Iximche itself. It's a beautiful historical park, and the ruins are indeed surrounded by ample forests, as well as by many sacred ceremonial sites. Much can be learned about Guatemala there, including that Iximche was the first capital of the country and that the word Quauhtemallan was transformed into name of the country. These are gifts from the Kaqchikels, a Kaqchikel woman told us.

Photo: Michal Zak/shutterstock.com

GUATEMALA– A LAND AS COLORFUL AND VARIED AS ITS WEAVING

Semuc Champey, Alta Verapaz.

"If you want to go quickly, walk slowly."

Guatemala, heart of the Maya world. Vivid, magical, mystical, and ancient. Its history dates back to the rise of the Maya civilization, whose legacy lives on today with the traditions and culture of its people.

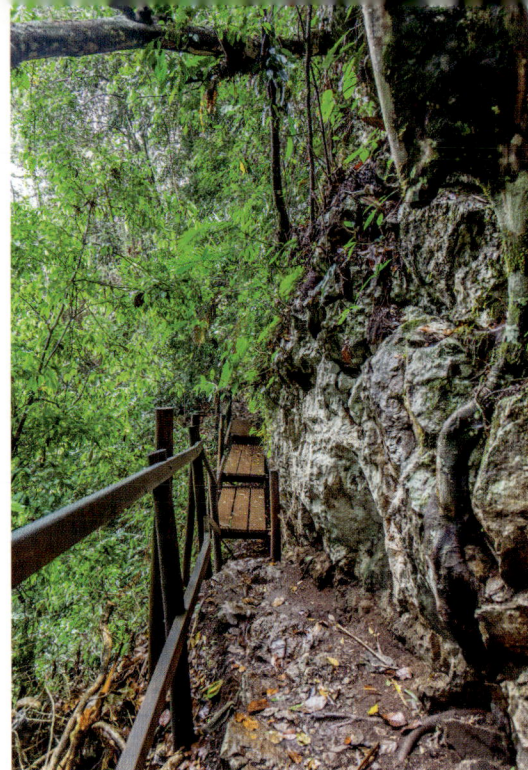

This page, clockwise from upper left: Santa Avelina Falls, San Juan Cotzal, Quiché; Semuc Champey; Ixil Triangle, Quiché; San Rafael, Rabinal, Baja Verapaz.

Opposite, clockwise from upper left: The road to Fuentes Georginas, Zunil, Quetzaltenango; Sa-mac, Cobán, Alta Verapaz; Posada de Santiago, Santiago Atitlán, Sololá; one of the ubiquitous buses to be seen all over the country; Santa Apolonia; La Vega, Santa Apolonia.

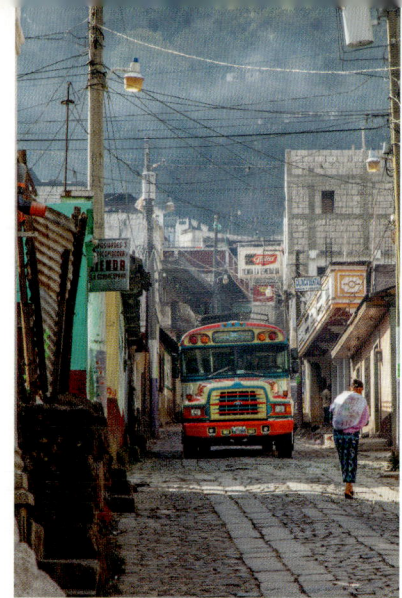

> *"Guatemala is color, color in all: its fruits, flowers, and vegetables; its homes, textiles and food; its mountains, lakes, and rivers; and its peoples' hopes and dreams."*

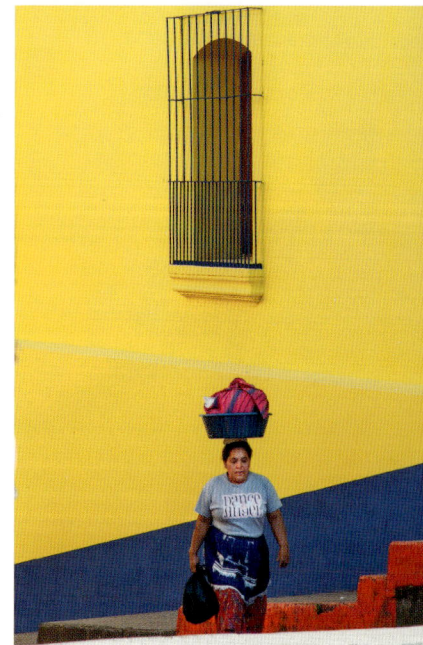

This page, clockwise from upper left: two views of Zunil, Quetzaltenango; two of Cobán, Alta Verapaz, Santa María Nebaj, Quiché; two more Zunil street scenes; San Gaspar Chajul, Quiché.

Opposite, clockwise from upper left: Rabinal; Santa Apolonia; Chichicastenango, Quiché; two market scenes in Zunil; Cobán, Alta Verapaz; two of Chichicastenango.

"Guatemala is a country where faith manifests itself everywhere, with ceremonies, rites, and hope—hope for a better future through effort, struggle, and work."

Opposite clockwise from upper left: Antigua; Zunil; Salama, Rabinal, Baja Verapaz; Quetzaltenango; National Cathedral in Guatemala City; Rabinal; San Andres Xecul, Totonicapan.

This page clockwise from upper left: Rabinal; San Gaspar Chajul; Momostenango, Totonicapan; two evening scenes in Quetzaltenango.

INTRODUCTION

My life of total immersion in all things weaving began in the late 1960s, and by the mid-1970s there was no going back. By the early 1990s there was hardly a job related to weaving or textiles that I had not had at some point: wholesaler, retailer, teacher of many kinds of students and classes, writer, administrator, production weaver, researcher of textile programs, consultant, and others, as well as playing an active role in multiple weavers guilds.

When I realized at one point that I did not know a single person who did not know how to weave I decided I needed to expand my horizons. At the age of forty I joined the Peace Corps and went to Honduras to work in water and sanitation. Upon my return, I moved from Colorado to Houston, where I worked for Pueblo to People, a fair trade organization that worked with artisans throughout Latin America.

My first trip to Guatemala was a field visit in 1992. Pueblo to People sold the work of hundreds of Guatemalan artisans, the bulk of it textiles. Teresa Cordón, a Guatemalan, was the field coordinator, and as such was my host for those two weeks. She took me east and west, north and south, to cities and rural areas, introducing me to the women and men whose work we sold.

What impressed me more than anything else on that trip was seeing Tere work with the people we encountered. With an ancient woman whose dedication was good but quality was lacking she was as gentle as a feather, using all the skills she had learned studying to be a teacher to constructively help the woman understand what was needed. With everyone she was clear, in a manner that was friendly but firm, on the need for quality, giving them the respect of focusing on the work, not on their need for work. Her relationships with the artisans were always built on mutual respect, treating each person as if they could do good work, could live up to their own potential. And so they did.

Creating *Traditional Weavers of Guatemala: Their Stories, Their Lives* with Tere as my co-author has been its own kind of adventure. Here we introduce you to twenty artisans—twelve weavers, three embroiderers, two spinners, one *jaspe* tier, one netter/looper, and one basket maker. Fourteen are women, six men, ranging in age from thirty-three to eighty-nine. Nineteen are Maya, one Ladino (not Maya). To converse with them we traveled to nine departments (like states or provinces), traversed altitudes from 770 to 2,770 meters (2,500 to 9,000 feet), conversed in eight languages besides English (with interpreters as needed), drove right to the front doors of some and hiked beyond where our four-wheel-drive vehicle would go for others. Although we knew some of these people before this project began, the stories shared here all come from conversations we had in 2012, 2013, and 2014. Both of us were present for every conversation, each bringing her own knowledge and understanding to the experience.

While of course we asked them questions, as much as possible, we encouraged them to tell us their stories as they remembered them, the parts of their lives that we would not have known to ask about. *And that leads to one of the most important things you need to know when reading this book. These are the stories of the women and men as they told them to us, as they do indeed remember them. The timing of events, or the events themselves, may match "historical fact," or may not. And that does not matter to us. What we wanted to know and want to share with you is their own world, in their own words.*

Conversing with them was an honor, a privilege, and a treat as well. To hear Don Domingo talk about taking care of the family cows eighty years ago, or Catarina and Susana state in no uncertain terms that a woman has to have self-respect, or see Amalia's face as she describes her surprise at the birth of her son a month early—while she was in Santa Fe at the International Folk Art Market ... these stories would not have come from a set of stock questions

Every person in this book has suffered terrible losses, and every one of them is an inspiration in how they have kept on living.

We did not look for such people, we were simply looking for textile artisans. With twenty out of twenty being so extraordinary, did the fates deliver something special to us or are these qualities inherent in their cultures—as Guatemalans, as Maya, and/or as textile artisans?

Guatemala is a beautiful country, as you will see throughout the book in Joe Coca's stunning photography. That the artisans and their textiles are also beautiful shines throughout as well. What we hope you will gain from the stories is the beginning of an understanding of a world probably very different from your own. It is a world that began in the time before time, a world

The southern half of Guatemala is a continuation of the Sierra Madre Ranges, an area so mountainous that much of it is still inaccessible by road.

where the phrase "fairly recently, in the last hundred years" makes sense. Just as mutual respect is the foundation of the relationship Tere has always had with the artisans she has known, so we believe that mutual respect between cultures is the foundation of a stronger and healthier world. Understanding, even just a glimmer, is the first step.

Deborah Chandler
Guatemala City
March 2015

Chapter 1

CECILIA CIRIN CHACACH
Saquitacaj, San José Poaquil, Chimaltenango
Kaqchikel

My favorite story about Cecilia Cirin, age fifty-nine, comes from her childhood. Her father had livestock—cattle, sheep, goats, and horses. The horses were pack animals, and Cecilia remembers their taking charcoal to the market in Guatemala City. Cecilia was on one horse, her father on another, and five more horses carried charcoal. They headed toward the city, a two-day ride away, and spent the first night in Chimaltenango (now a 45-minute trip in a pickup). They arrived in the city on the second day, and for the next few days sold the charcoal in the market. Although the trip back still took two days, those days were easier, and they moved faster with the pack horses traveling light.

Growing up, Cecilia had many of the chores and learned the lessons of all girls in her world: herding the animals, breaking the cornstalks to speed the drying process, carrying lunch and water (in a *tinaja*, a clay jug on her head) to her father and brothers (which is when she met her best friend, Emeteria), grinding corn on a *piedra de moler* (grinding stone made of volcanic rock), and cooking. And, of course, spinning, weaving, and dyeing. By the time she was thirteen, she was adept at all of those tasks.

Sadly, the year she turned thirteen, her father died of an illness. Her three sisters were already married, and her three brothers were already drunks, so it fell to Cecilia and her mother to tend to everything. Then, when Cecilia was just fifteen, her mother died of an illness. And because fifteen-year-old girls could not live alone, she got married and moved from the town of San José Poaquil to the nearby *aldea* (village) of Saquitacaj, where Emeteria lived also.

The aldea where Cecilia lives is about 3 kilometers (1.9 miles) from San José Poaquil, which is about a half-hour drive from San Juan Comalapa. In the early days of political boundaries, the 1800s and beyond, Poaquil was part of the *municipio* (county, the most important political subdivision in Guatemala) of Comalapa, as were San Martin Jilotepeque, and Santa Apolonia. Not until the 1890s did the towns break off to become their own municipios, and by then the patterns of the women's huipils, patterns unique to each area, had long since been well established. San Martin was a center of weaving for the area, with the weavers selling many of their textiles to other communities, and thus influencing the local designs. Comalapa was the political and market center, and many ideas spread from there. The huipils of Poaquil were, and still are, nearly identical to those of Comalapa, with noticeable influence from San Martin. Those influences—in part—explain the complexity of the Poaquil huipil, which is also the huipil of Saquitacaj and other aldeas around Poaquil.

Complexity hardly begins to describe these huipils, each of which has most, if not all, of the following weave structures:

Warp-faced plain weave
Weft-faced plain weave
Creya (unique red stripe), pick and pick, or mixed designs
Single-faced brocade
Double-sided brocade

Right: Gathering every weekend to weave and just be together is a near-sacred ritual for Cecilia, her daughters, daughter-in-law, and granddaughters.

Red creya stripe, with
narrow striped and
dotted bands. Weft-face
plain weave.

Double-sided brocade.
Note the weft floats on
the back.

Single-faced brocade.
The back is black, with
no floats.

Punteado. Small
floats of color on
the front, occasional
small weft floats on
the back.

Warp-faced plain
weave. Note that both
panels of this huipil
have four selvedges.

These narrow stripes
are called separators.

This is a huipil woven "by the hand of a woman."
When a huipil is woven on a draw loom, it is
said to be woven "by the hand of a man" and
is less valuable.

Double- or two-faced brocade
Balanced plain-weave
Marcador
Semi-marcador
Punteado

The neck, after being turned in and stitched, is then embellished—with embroidery, a beaded edging, and other techniques.

Those are the weave structures and techniques. The materials may include any or all of the following: various kinds of cotton, acrylic for warmth, rayon, silk, or metallic threads; and for the neck, velvet, beads, or other trims.

Creya, the red shoulder stripe that distinguishes the Comalapa and Poaquil huipil, is named for a cotton yarn called crea that was imported from Europe. Perhaps the most impressive thing about the creya is that it is a weft-faced stripe woven on a warp-faced warp. A very fine weft is used for the stripe, one so fine that it may take an hour to weave an inch. For a period of time, the red stripe was woven with blue, but now red is more common once again. Not all Poaquil huipils have the red stripe, but many do. By all accounts but one, the red stripe has no symbolic significance. The one exception comes from Gaby, one of Cecilia's daughters, who has studied in the city as well as in the village. She told us that the red stripe represents discrimination against and physical abuse of women.

Cecilia, her daughters, and daughter-in-law all still wear *traje* (traditional clothing) because they are more comfortable in it. While they showed us their huipils, they discussed trends, saying that there are fashion changes every year. The base cloth color changes, separator stripes get wider or narrower, and the images become bigger or smaller. The images can be animals, flowers of vastly different styles, flower baskets and vases, little human figures, cupids, and a wonderful variety of geometric shapes. The colors can be strong or soft, solid or *manchado* (space-dyed), and more or less background may show through. And though the elements that have been included from San Martin are there, the huipils are clearly distinct. Finally, in spite of what seems like endless variation, it is still possible to identify a huipil from Poaquil or Comalapa amid all the other huipils in Guatemala.

Cecilia and her husband, Manuel Gonzalez Ovalle, started their family with four daughters, working their land. They grew vegetables and raised fowl and other animals. They were close to Manuel's parents, who were bread bakers in Poaquil, and their daughter Ana went to live with her grandparents when she was two. Even though the roads were barely in existence, one of their proudest possessions was a car. Life was good.

During those years, part of Cecilia's work was to clothe her family using her loom. She bought raw white cotton in the market and brought it home to spin on a supported spindle, then sometimes dyed it with local plants. To weave her huipils, she used that yarn as well as commercial yarn. After she had woven enough for her household, which required far more cloth than the huipils for herself and her daughters, Cecilia would weave to sell, earning a little extra income for the family.

Meanwhile, her friend Emeteria lived just houses away, was also married, and also had four children. The two women continued to have a strong bond, which became an anchor in the storm about to hit them.

On Christmas Eve in 1981, Cecilia and her family were at home. At 7:00 p.m., the *Judiciales* (the most vicious division of the police) arrived at their door. They took Manuel away, along with everything they could steal, which was everything, leaving Cecilia and the girls home alone, with nothing. Not far away, they also took Emeteria's husband, and took her as well, putting her in the local jail. They burned everything, leaving her small children behind to fend for themselves.

Emeteria came home after three days. On the fourth day, they found Manuel's body on the highway near Sumpango, some 32 kilometers (20 miles) away, totally burned. They never found the body of Emeteria's husband. Four years later, as Manuel's father was walking down the street selling bread, the army handcuffed and took him away as well.

Thus ended that chapter of Cecilia's life. She and Emeteria were twenty-seven.

Cecilia Cirin was born in 1954, at a pivotal moment in the life of Guatemala. That year ended the "Golden Age" of Guatemala and began a time of internal unrest that lasted more than

To weave the two or three panels it takes to create a huipil so the patterns match at the seams, each panel is woven on a separate warp. Once the first one is completed it is held up beside the second as it is being woven, for reference. In this picture note the brown base of the basket on the bottom cloth.

forty years. By the time she was four years old, Cecilia had already lived through the rise and fall of six presidents, all military. She didn't know it at the time, of course.

Officially, the war lasted from 1960 to 1996, ending with the signing of peace accords between the military and the guerrillas. It was a dark time, and even those few who were not directly affected were living in a world filled with fear. Although the guerrillas are not totally innocent, in the end, the military was declared responsible for most of the violence. Some 200,000 people were killed or disappeared and many, many thousands more went into exile in Mexico, the United States, or anywhere else they could go to be safe. Those who could not get out of the country often hid in the mountains, subsisting on whatever they could find; many of those were children whose families had been killed.

In some cases, entire communities were targeted for destruction, so if some few did manage to escape, they needed to keep where they came from a secret. The fastest way to identify a woman from a distance is her huipil, and so many women had to shed their huipils for the first time in their lives. At the same time, when one is running for her life, packing huipils—or anything else—is not an option, so for that reason, too, women's clothing began to change. It takes three to six months to weave a huipil; to buy a huipil, one needs money and a market. These were not available to those on the run.

Opinions as to why some areas were hit harder than others are countless. Whatever the reasons, every town named so far in this story is included on the list of those hardest hit by army violence. (Artisans whose stories are included later in the book also live in areas on that list.) Many programs were developed to help war widows and orphans. *Tejidos Guadalupe*, with which Cecilia and Emeteria worked for five years, offered programs for 300 war widows and an orphanage that at its peak took care of 125 children. People told Cecilia that she should give up her children because she would obviously not be able to take care of them. Her response was, "Just because you have lost your husband doesn't mean you can't raise your children."

Sugar, bananas, coffee, and cardamom (and in the past, cotton) are considered the traditional crops of Guatemala, the biggest food crops for export. Of those, only bananas have had their own stable work force. The rest, being seasonal, survive by the work of migrants. Many people talk of going "to the coast," a phrase that doesn't necessarily refer to an area close to the coast but one that's lower in altitude. In some cases, whole families go; in others, only the father or the males or the older ones go. It depends on many factors, the primary one being what they have at home, such as

If this traditional Poaquil huipil had been woven on a draw loom (which is common), each color used would go all the way across the width of each panel. Because it was done on a backstrap loom, a color could be used in a very narrow space next to another color, as with the zigzags here. In this huipil only the yarns of the separator stripes go all the way across. All the rest were woven with small bundles of yarn, called butterflies, one for each color.

other jobs, small farms, babies, and aging parents. Considered by most to be a real home-breaker in terms of absence, migrant work is also a home-saver in terms of providing a badly needed income.

The conditions are tough, as they are for migrant workers anywhere. In Guatemala, the situation is complicated by being multilingual. There are twenty-two Mayan languages spoken in Guatemala, as well as Xinca, Garifuna, and Spanish, which means that many of the migrant workers cannot speak with each other. Some *fincas* (large farms, plantations) send trucks to bring people from farther inland at the beginning of the season and return them at the end. Other people come and go on their own. Some go with pre-set contracts, others go looking for work. There is no single story.

In Cecilia and Emeteria's case, migrant work saved them. From October through January of 1983 and 1984, they went to a coffee finca, taking their children with them. They very quickly learned that they could do better making tortillas for the other workers than picking coffee themselves, so that became their work, starting at 1 a.m. every morning. They also made wicker baskets for the pickers to use, which they sold for ten cents each. Thinking about that time, Cecilia would smile. "It was good. Our children had enough food then."

"Weaving was a necessity," Cecilia says, but I also loved it. I sold some, but mostly I wove for my family."

A home has more textiles than simply clothing. In a world without disposables, consider towels for both kitchen and body, cloth to cover food, diapers, baby carriers, head protectors (from rain or sun), market bags, bedding, and much more. Clothing for

Left: Even babies wear traje. Note that the neck of the baby's huipil is not round or straight but sewn in Vs all the way around. Her cousin's huipil is from Patzun, not Poaquil; wearing huipils from other communities is quite common now. Most interesting is the baby's hat. It is made by sewing a rectangular cloth into a tube and gathering the top to close it. Not as elastic as a knit cap, it is nevertheless quite common and keeps babies' heads warm just fine.

Right: The monochromatic mix of colors in each figure comes from yarn called manchado, in this case translating as dyed with several colors, or space-dyed. This pattern is woven in Poaquil but originated in San Martin Jilotepeque.

the girls and women includes huipils, of course. The skirts, called *corte,* are usually woven on foot looms. *Fajas* (belts) are backstrap woven. *Sobrehuipiles* (over-huipils) are a far more elaborate and fine version of the usual huipil, with the distinction that they are longer, wider, and often lightweight. They're worn over the top of the daily huipil and corte for special ceremonies. There was never a time when Cecilia had nothing to weave.

Also during that time, Cecilia wove and sold huipils. She figured out that what she earned selling three huipils gave her enough money to pay for help with her own harvest. She still had the land her husband had left her, but the oldest of her four daughters was only nine when her father was killed, so the girls were too small to do much farm work just yet. Besides, it was time for them to learn to weave, which they did.

Three years after Manuel was killed, Cecilia married Marcelo Quin Velasquez, a vegetable wholesaler whose wife had died of an illness some time earlier. As a *comerciante* (commercial business-man), his success had inspired some jealousy in someone and, as was common, he was picked up by the soldiers and tortured for three days. He was then released. He continued as a comerciante, and in his and Cecilia's twenty-four years together, they had four more children, three girls and one boy, making seven girls and one boy altogether. The family believes that when Marcelo died of headaches in 2009, it may have been in part from the long-term effects of the three days of torture. (Emeteria, who also remarried, had eight children, seven boys and one girl.)

Over the years, Cecilia's health has deteriorated. She has not been able to weave for some time because of poor eyesight and a bad back. She has aches and pains all over, and now her hearing is bothering her. All of that makes life more difficult, but it is not her highest priority. As has been true since the very beginning, keeping her family strong is the focus of Cecilia's life. Of her eight children, who now range in age from twenty to forty, six daughters live close by, in the same village, and are in and out of her house constantly. Of those six, one is the widow of an alcoholic husband; she has six children. The other five are married and also

have children.

Cecilia cries, missing the other two children. Her only son, now twenty-eight, has been gone ten years, living in the United States. He sends money back to Cecilia and his wife and daughter, who live with Cecilia. He and his wife are building a new house, attached to Cecilia's; when he comes back, that will be their home.

Cecilia's daughter Ana Maria works in Guatemala City. You will meet her later in this book. Ana's son Manuel, thirteen, lives with Cecilia. Ana works as a live-in domestic, and her last couple of jobs have not allowed for Manuel to live with her. Raising a son costs money, as Cecilia knows, and so while she is very sad to have Ana so far away (a four-hour bus ride), she knows that it is necessary. Like her brother, Ana also helps support Cecilia, and in her case that includes the use of land and animals that she owns in the village. Thanks to cell phones and family gatherings, Cecilia has not lost all contact with Ana, but she does miss her and wishes she lived in Saquitacaj with the rest of the family. (So does Ana.)

Because everyone is sad that Cecilia lives alone—meaning that none of her daughters lives with her—they have family gatherings every weekend, for general togetherness and also to weave together. Ana can only get to the gatherings every other weekend. Then, she revels at being with everyone, especially her son, whom she misses terribly. They all look forward to the day when their brother can be with them, too.

Cecilia Cirin is a monument to resilience and strength. Rising above impossible situations, determined to keep her family intact, this is a woman who understands what it means to be alive. Cecilia's daughters dote on her, giving her all the love and attention they can. It is clear that they adore her. Emeteria, with her own painful aging body, still lives a few doors away. The two women continue to be best friends, the one constant in each other's lives for more than half a century. After losing both of her parents when she was so young, Cecilia has spent her life striving to maintain what she values most: above all else, family. In spite of formidable odds, she has achieved her goal.

HOGARES SANTA MARÍA DE GUADALUPE AND TEJIDOS GUADALUPE
SANTA APOLONIA AND SAN JOSÉ POAQUIL

In 1985, The School Sisters of St. Francis, based in Milwaukee, Wisconsin, opened Hogares Santa María de Guadalupe in Santa Apolonia. It's an orphanage for children who lost one or both parents to the Armed Conflict. Chepito, age seven, became the first new family member. Julio, age one, came second. At its peak, Hogares had 125 children, all from within a radius of 15 kilometers (9 miles). Often in sibling groups, the children were brought in by family members, neighbors, godparents, or others who knew they needed help. Other children, abandoned or orphaned, were sent by the children's court. Designated a "permanent population," the children came as infants through age eight and stayed until they were eighteen. At the age of ten, they chose the way they would contribute to the orphanage family. They then began to learn such skills as sewing, repairing shoes, or carpentering. And, of course, they went to school.

Equally compelling were the hundreds of war widows who suddenly needed a source of income. Because virtually all of them were weavers, the Sisters began a second project at the orphanage, Tejidos Guadalupe (*Tejidos*—weavings, handwoven cloth). The women produced the work in their homes. Although some woven pieces were finished when they arrived, most went to the sewing workshop to be made into finished goods, such as coin purses, bags, and placemats. The many products were displayed in the orphanage, where visitors from the United States or other countries would buy what they could, often taking them home to sell to raise money for the orphanage. Later, the project was moved to the neighboring town of San José Poaquil. Participation in Tejidos Guadalupe peaked at 300 women, all from within that same 15 kilometer (9 mile) radius.

Both programs still exist, and both have changed with the times. Now, the orphanage's children come exclusively through the courts and arrive from all over the country. Tejidos Guadalupe participants still weave and sew, and in addition, the organization offers programs about medicinal herbs, vegetable gardens, small livestock breeding, microcredit, and more.

And Chepito and Julio, now grown men? Chepito lives in Poaquil and works with his uncle doing agricultural work and selling in the market. Julio lives with his wife and children in Chimaltenango and has recently reunited with the sisters he had not seen since they were separated as children.

Photo by the authors

Chapter 2

EUGENIA TEPAZ LÓPEZ
La Vega, Santa Apolonia, Chimaltenango
Kaqchikel

In a document dated June 18, 1689, Fray Francisco de Zuaza makes reference to "Indian potters of all kinds of crockery.... The men take the clay to their homes and the women produce the articles, the sale of which helps support the family."

Eugenia Tepaz López, fifty-nine, was one of eight siblings born into a family of potters. Low-fire ceramics, the kind used to make *comales* (the slightly curved griddles for making tortillas and toasting coffee beans), *ollas* (cooking pots), *tinajas* (narrow-necked jugs for carrying water), *malacates* (drop spindles for spinning thread, made with a clay ball at the bottom end of a stick), and for fun, whistles and small animals—that was the work of the family.

Eugenia, however, did not want to work with clay. She preferred cloth and wanted to embroider huipils. Her mother was neutral on the subject, but her father was outright opposed. Nevertheless, she persisted, and at thirteen she started studying her mother's and other women's huipils and taught herself "to count (embroider)," as she puts it. Her father never relented, and in fact forbade her to even wear the local huipil. She never gave in either and is now considered the premier huipil maker in Santa Apolonia. Meanwhile, with the arrival of aluminum cookware, plastic water jugs, commercially spun thread, and every kind of whistle and toy, ceramics activity in the area has all but disappeared.

Embroidery is one of two design elements that distinguish the huipils of Santa Apolonia from the backstrap-woven huipils that are typical of most of the highlands. The embroidery technique is actually called "false brocade" because it looks so much like some kinds of brocaded backstrap cloth. The second unique characteristic is the placement of the design: all of the design work is on the back. From the front, one sees a woman in a plain white top with a fine edging around the neck. It is not until she is walking away that the extraordinary artistry and beauty are visible. No one we could find knows the why of either design element: embroidery instead of weaving or beauty on the back only.

Backstrap-woven huipils consist of two or three panels that are woven first, then sewn together. With a lot of skill and a little luck, the designs in each panel match up. The Santa Apolonia huipil is first sewn and then embroidered, so the stitching goes right across the seam; there is no matching up to be done.

"We go to the market in Tecpan to buy *manta* (flour sack–like cloth), which comes from weavers in Totonicapan. We always look for the best-quality cloth. We also buy our thread there, at the market, or at stores on nonmarket days. We use *sedalina* (DMC perle cotton #8). Each little ball costs 5 quetzales (Q. 5) (about $.65) and it takes forty balls to make a traditional huipil."

The colors are like a rainbow, with every bright color you can think of. These days, the younger women are asking to have some of the design on the front and changes in the colors. We asked Eugenia if that was offensive. "No, it's fine," she responded. She says that older women still ask for all the colors. They might ask for a little more of one color, like more yellow or more blue, but they still want the whole rainbow. The younger women may ask for a mix of blues, or burgundy and blue, or some other mix that appeals to them. "Anything is fine. I'll make what anyone asks for."

We asked if she has a favorite color. She began fondly picking up little balls and naming them. "No, I like them all: blue, green, red, yellow... I think I like the turquoise best because it goes

Right: Eugenia Tepaz López—from obstinate daughter to most respected embroiderer in the community.

Traditionally all of the embroidery was done on the back of the garments, as shown in the insets. It is rare to find a woman wearing a Santa Apolonia huipil for everyday use, perhaps because it is so difficult to keep it clean.

country, from barely noticeable to whole mountainsides collapsing, are a constant reality during those months. Given that the runoff coming down the sides of the ravine is in no way directed or controlled, mudslides are common in La Vega. One such slide, in June 2012, closed the highway and affected seventy-five homes.

Eugenia's home is typical of the area, in both architecture and activity. Two rows of rooms, each with a roofed corridor running across the front, face each other over an open patio filled with dogs and chickens and children. A similar home some 50 yards away and uphill houses extended family. Behind one row of rooms is a carpenter shop; behind the other is a little *tienda* (a tiny shop that sells basic daily needs; such shops are ubiquitous in rural and urban areas alike).

Eugenia and her husband, Francisco, had seven children. Of their three daughters, one died at age thirty-two of headaches, the other two live close by, helping Eugenia "count" as needed. Of their four sons, two work in agriculture with their father and two

went to the United States to find work. Of the two who left, one is now happy to be home again working in the carpenter shop; the other is still in the United States.

Francisco has always been supportive of his wife's work. It has provided seed money, literally, for his farming, cash flow when he needed it. But even more, he said, "She is happy doing the work and that makes me happy." Given her advanced age of fifty-nine, Eugenia's children think she should quit working and relax. "After all this time, aren't you bored with it?" they ask. Her answer is simple. "I like what I am doing, and it makes me happy. I'll work as long as I can."

CHIMALTENANGO AND THE 1976 EARTHQUAKE

"Beneath one of the most beautiful landscapes in the world—the volcanic mountains and lapidary lakes of highland Guatemala—lurks a perennial menace: the tectonic plates, whose periodic clashes bring devastation to the country. The years 1773, 1816, and 1902 are recalled for their legacy of death and damage, but they were exceeded in our time by the disaster that struck Guatemala early in the morning of February 4, 1976. It is recorded that within 39 seconds 23,000 people had died, 76,000 were injured, and whole towns were leveled to the ground." James C. Langley, Ancestry and Artistry Maya Textiles from Guatemala, Textile Museum of Canada, 2013.

Chimal—shield, tenango—place of: Chimaltenango, the place of the shield

There are some things you just can't be shielded from.

Although it was not the epicenter, Chimaltenango was one of the areas hardest hit by the earthquake that affected more than half the country. Three municipios were completely flattened and the departmento (state) had the highest number of deaths, almost 14,000.

The immediate devastation is incomprehensible. The long-term effects, while blessedly less dramatic, are also deep and wide. In the past, driving through the countryside, you would see a postcard-perfect scene of adobe houses with red-tile roofs surrounded by green cornfields. Because the weight of falling tiles killed thousands of people, the roofs are now corrugated sheet metal, soon rusty. Adobe was once the building material of choice for many, even when other materials were within reach. But the thick adobe walls that fell during the earthquake proved fatal for thousands. Now, there are more and more concrete block houses. (Note: Guatemalan concrete blocks are much lighter than those made in the United States.) New building codes don't show, but multi-story buildings in the cities are far safer now.

But none of those things can fill a space where a town was and now is not. Just gone. In the town of Santa Apolonia the cemetery itself was so damaged that it could not be used, so a new one was created, with mass graves for hundreds or thousands of earthquake victims. Today a small protected area survives, with a few headstones –most with the date February 4, 1976.

One positive element of disasters anywhere is how people come together. They join forces, helping each other in extraordinary ways; it is the best humanity has to offer. Then-President Kjell Laugerud captured a sense of the people's resilience when he said, "Guatemala is wounded, but not to death."

Photo by the authors

Chapter 3

HERMINIA SANTOS

San Antonio Aguas Calientes, Sacatepequez
Kaqchikel

"… the weaving from [San Antonio] Aguas Calientes is amazingly fine in detail and beautifully done."
— Mary Meigs Atwater

"I wove nonstop for sixty years, and now I can't for the pain. That's hard. I love to weave, and I weave to sell. The two cannot be separated; they are equally important," Herminia tells us. "So I weave a little bit, keep the store going. I can sell things other family members weave. I hope the treatments I'm getting will help." (Herminia's daughter-in-law adds, "It drives her crazy to not be able to weave.")

When Herminia Santos was seven years old, her mother died, so her grandmother raised her. When Herminia was eight, her grandmother taught her to weave. When she was twelve, she started to sell her weaving. At the age of thirteen, she had her one and only year of school. At sixteen, she got married and started her family of seven children. Now sixty-nine, Herminia has been married for fifty-three years to Chavelo, a kind and good man who clearly adores her. "We did not spend a lot of money on things we did not need. We used it to put our children through school. But we had a big party for our fiftieth anniversary. It was fun."

When Herminia and Chavelo were growing up, Kaqchikel was the language spoken in their homes. Going to school was difficult because they didn't speak Spanish. They were determined that their own children would learn Spanish right from the start. So although they still spoke Kaqchikel to each other, they spoke only Spanish to their children, making it the home language. Now, the tides have shifted again, and they wish they had made sure their children were fluent in both. As it is, their daughter speaks both languages; their sons understand Kaqchikel but don't speak it well. It's a challenge faced by indigenous (and other) people everywhere: how to maintain one culture while functioning in another.

Some traditions are easier to keep than others. In many Maya communities, it is the custom that a girl about to marry a young man will weave a *tzute* for her soon-to-be mother-in-law. A tzute is a cloth that serves a wide variety of purposes: it's a head covering to protect from sun or rain, a carrying cloth for going to or coming from the market, and a leveling cloth for carrying baskets or boxes on one's head. Not big enough to carry a baby on a woman's back, it is big enough to wipe away tears or spilled Coke, to clean off a table before eating, to protect a sleeping child from sun or dust or bugs, and to serve a dozen other uses. There are ceremonial tzutes as well, for men as well as women, which are generally worn folded on the head or draped over one shoulder. For a daughter-in-law to bestow such a gift on her mother-in-law is a recognition of both the work and the beauty of life, a good start. Herminia has four daughters-in-law. Three of them gave her tzutes they had woven for her; the fourth gave her a huipil, also woven for her. These textiles are beautiful both in and of themselves and also as representatives of San Antonio Aguas Calientes, a town known especially for its fine weaving.

In addition to their stunning beauty, what sets the textiles of San Antonio apart is one of the techniques used to weave them. Developed as recently as the 1930s, double-sided patterns, also called *marcador*, are completely reversible, with the front and back being virtually identical. (Both words, *double-sided* and *marcador*, are used in other ways in other places.) The technique referred to here is a kind of weft-faced tapestry in which the weft goes over-under-over-under groups of four warps, over and back, then has a plain weave weft between each two pattern wefts. (It's much more complicated than this description suggests.) The technique was developed especially for the total freedom of design it allows, and to take advantage of the arrival of new design ideas from Europe

Taking time for the chores of life, it took Herminia a year to weave this fully marca-dor huipil. She says that a well-cared-for huipil can last forty years.

This tzute—an all-purpose cloth that can be for daily or ceremonial use—is totally reversible, with the same birds and flowers on both sides. You can tell that first, because it comes from San Antonio Aguas Calientes, and second, for the curves in the designs.

Above: On this huipil there are at least six stripes woven using different techniques. The weavers of San Antonio Aguas Calientes have an extensive library of patterns in their heads and hands.

Left: When Herminia opened her store to help support the family, she started by selling what she had on hand. A weaver's house is full of handwoven textiles used for every purpose imaginable.

Herminia at home, always with fresh flowers.

in the form of pre-printed cross-stitch embroidery patterns.

There are no rules about how much area is covered by single-sided or double-sided techniques, or where each is located. Either technique might be used only on the shoulders of a huipil, in stripes around the chest, for the body but not the shoulders, or for the entire huipil. It's easy to recognize which parts are single-sided and which are double-sided. The single-sided parts are made up of geometric patterns—zigzags, diagonals, straight lines, and diamonds. The double-sided areas have images with curves—birds, flowers, fish. The double-sided weaving takes much longer and uses more yarn; therefore, it's more costly to produce. For that reason, fewer and fewer huipils are being created completely in the two-sided technique, which today would likely sell for Q. 3,000 to Q. 7,000, or about $400 to $900.

The huipil that Herminia is wearing in these photographs is fully two-sided. Among the other activities of her life, this huipil

took her a year to weave. "If you take good care of it, a huipil can last forty years," she told us, so a good huipil is a good investment.

"We had the blessing of having a special child, one with *la-bio leporino* (harelip). We needed money for his surgery, so my husband, Chavelo, agreed that I could start selling my weavings again. I started with whatever textiles I could find around the house. The first day I sold a *servilleta* (another all-purpose cloth, smaller than a tzute) for Q. 15 (about $2). That was 1967 or so. I've had my store for forty-five years now."

Herminia's store is in Antigua, where it has been for the past twenty-five years. Before that, she had a store in San Antonio for twenty years. The two towns are 8 kilometers (5 miles) and worlds apart.

Antigua is a beautiful colonial city that is the heart and soul of Guatemala. Because it's fairly close to Guatemala City, many people flying into the country, from backpackers to visiting dignitaries, go there first. The *Semana Santa* (Easter or Holy Week) processions are legendary. Antigua is home to dozens of language schools, bringing in budding Spanish speakers from all over the world. Flattened by earthquakes on several occasions over the last three hundred years, the city's ruins are part of the charm and at least partly responsible for the city being a United Nations Education, Scientific, and Cultural Organization (UNESCO) World Heritage Site.

Herminia's store is in the market where the local people go to buy shoes, hammers, and toothpaste. It's a big market, and outsiders wander in as well, so there are also textiles and other artisan-created items that local people are more likely to sell than buy. Herminia's store has a mix of textiles, from high-end huipils to inexpensive coin purses and key chains. Her location seems hidden in the labyrinth, but people do find her, including repeat buyers from other countries who know she has or can get some very special pieces. We talked about her store and how it works.

"We used to work with weavers on a special-order basis, giving them a deposit so they could buy the yarn, the rest to be paid when they delivered the finished piece," Herminia tells us. "But too often they took the deposit and never came back. So we quit working that way and now only pay for finished pieces."

"Buyers sometimes want pieces that have more two-sided work, but they want old huipils, not new ones. And they usually don't want to pay what a full two-sided huipil costs," she muses.

"I wove and sold my work in the store all the time until two

Herminia's mother died when she was very young, so she grew up with her grandmother. This little piece is a scrap from a huipil woven by Herminia's *abuela*.

years ago," she recalls. "Then I started having terrible pains in my back and legs, and now I can only weave for a few minutes at a time. I'm getting some treatment and take pain pills, but I still hurt. My husband left his job in construction so he could help me in the store." (Note: Chavelo was seventy when he quit his construction job.)

When Herminia was growing up, huipils were woven with bright colors, and the base cloth could be any color. Then, the style changed to softer colors and only a black base cloth. Now it is moving back to bright colors and any color of background again. Style changes don't happen swiftly, of course, so it is easy to see both soft and bright colors walking the streets at the same time. When Herminia spoke of changes in fashion and other events that affected sales, she gave us a question and answer rolled into one: "How did I decide what to weave? I wove what would sell."

Of Herminia and Chavelos's seven children, two died young, leaving four sons and one daughter. One son died at age forty-two of diarrhea, so now they have three sons, four daughters-in-law, their daughter, her husband, sixteen grandchildren, and seven great-grandchildren.

The most important success of Herminia and Chavelo's life is that all of their children graduated from school and are now professionals. They also managed to invest in land, so now each family has a home as well. The couple has an apartment built in the back of the house of one of their sons, so that when they die, the space will revert to him automatically. All are in San Antonio Aguas Calientes—another good thing.

There is a belief that a home with doves is one of peace and harmony. Seeing the doves in Herminia and Chavelo's home, looking at their impressive home-altar, listening to them talk of what is most important, and doing so with affection for each other, it would appear that the doves are in the right house.

In the end, the warmth of home is what it's all for.

Chapter 4

LOLA SAPALÚ

Santiago Atitlán, Sololá
Tz'utujil

"The cloth lives an experience."

—Lola Sapalú

As handspun yarns were replaced by commercial yarns, the work of spinning and weaving gradually changed. With fewer hours devoted to spinning, the women had more time to weave. In addition, with less texture coming from the yarn itself, the cloth seemed to beg for more designs to make up for that loss. Nowhere is that shift more obvious than in the huipils of Santiago Atitlán. Earlier styles were visually simple, the patterning coming from colored warp stripes, and sometimes weft stripes formed by both color and a brocade technique special to Atitlán. Those huipils had no embroidery on the body; they might have had some around the neck, but not necessarily. The main cloth was white.

Leap ahead to the present, and you wouldn't even know you were in the same town. The base cloth may still be white, but it is just as likely to be a soft blue or lavender. The warp and weft stripes are still there, but now they often create little squares that serve as frames for embroidery. And therein lies the difference— embroidery.

By now Santiago Atitlán is famous for its embroidery, a well-deserved recognition. But the advent of embroidery is recent enough, dating back a hundred years or so, to be tied to the change from handspun to commercially spun yarn. Cantel, the first spinning mill in Guatemala, was built in 1876. The earliest embroidered huipils had very little embroidery, as if the embroiderers themselves were testing the waters. With time and acceptance, the area covered by embroidery grew along with shifts in style, and now it is not uncommon to see huipils, gorgeous huipils, with so much embroidery that the base cloth is relegated to a background status, or at times not visible at all. Some designs use those little squares to frame small figures, most often birds or Mayan glyphs. Some have birds flying in rows, over the vertical stripes and between the horizontal stripes. Others go all out, with birds flying all over the huipil regardless of where any lines might be. Some are even woven without lines because the embroidery is so profuse that any stripes would never be seen anyway.

Taking all those options into account (and there are more), it's a marvel to walk down the street in Atitlán. All of those styles and variations are there, a feast for the eyes as well as an education.

None of those changes—from handspun to commercial yarn, from simplicity to profusion in design, and from weaving alone to weaving plus embroidery—fell out of the sky. Over the course of the entire century, every one of them came from someone who was both talented enough and brave enough to risk "going public" with new ideas. An innovator. An artist. A Lola Sapalú.

Lola's mother taught each of her eight daughters to embroider at age eight and to weave at age ten. (Their one brother learned other things.) Lola, now fifty-eight, likes weaving and feels that she can be creative with it, but she loves embroidery best. "With embroidery, I can use my imagination. I have a lot of designs in my head." And not only in her head. Evidence of Lola's ideas and innovations abound.

In most schools in Guatemala, both public and private, students wear school uniforms. They may also have special clothing to honor special events. One of the ways Lola shares her talent is

First the cloth is woven. Multiple heddle sticks are used to create the zigzags of the horizontal lines; it is a style of brocade nearly unique to the area of Santiago Atitlán. Then the panels are sewn together, and finally they are embroidered. All the pointed designs around the neck are embroidered, as are all the birds and flowers.

to design huipils for schools. For both uniforms and special-event huipils, she creates several designs, one is chosen, and then the mothers make the huipils for their daughters.

Lola says she likes sharing her ideas. The only thing she does not like is when someone takes a design and produces it in great quantities cheaply—and she gets no credit.

Lola-as-Artist has clearly been enhanced by her partnership with her husband, the equally well-known artist Manuel Reanda. Manuel is and has always been a painter. Lola first saw him when she was twelve; it was love at first sight. At thirteen, she spoke to him for the first time. When she was sixteen and he was twenty-one, his mother asked her parents if the two could get married. One stumbling block was that Lola's family came from an agricultural life and it took some time before they were comfortable with the idea of her marrying an artist. Nevertheless, the traditional rituals ensued, and they began their life together. Lola and Manuel have now been together for more than forty years, and their love for each other and their mutual respect as artists

Whereas woven threads can go only vertically or horizontally, embroidered threads can go in any direction, allowing total freedom of design.

are abundantly clear.

The strength of their relationship and their religious faith have played important roles in their lives. When she was two and a half years old, Sonia, the first of their four children, fell and fractured her skull. Permanent damage to her brain and one arm resulted. Even though she will never be able to live on her own, she is able to live a comfortable life and is happy. Manuel says that before the accident, he was more driven, pushing at life. Sonia's accident reminded him of what is important in life, a lesson that has never left him. The couple is involved in their church and feels close to God. Recently, one of their sons married a girl from the next town over. Both her heritage and her religion were different from his, but they saw no problem. "It's all the same God, and as long as she loves him it's fine."

Lola recognizes spirituality of other kinds, too. When her mother was teaching Lola and her sisters to weave and embroider, part of the lesson was that their materials are sacred and should be treated accordingly. Keeping yarn or thread in a basket is fine, for instance, but you need to avoid putting another basket close by. If you put them too close, the spirit (or sprite) of the second basket will get into the first and tangle the yarns. Lola showed us a warp she was setting up as proof of the warning. She had a jaspe (ikat) warp stripe that had tangled and had to be replaced, no easy task on a backstrap loom. Lola knows that not everyone would believe these things, but it has been her experience so she does.

Lola had her first exhibition at *Bellas Artes* (Beautiful Arts) in Guatemala City when she was eighteen years old. She sold her first huipil there for Q. 100 (about $13). A few years ago, the Antigua store Nim P'ot hosted another exhibition, this time a twenty-five year retrospective of her work. Last year, she sold a huipil for Q. 3,800 (about $500). (The local market price for huipils in Atitlán is now between Q. 500 and Q. 1,500, or about $65 to $200.)

She proudly shared with us her contributions to the evolution of Atitlán huipils, which include using lavender as the base cloth, embroidering around the sleeves, finding ever new and creative ways to incorporate beads, using jaspe stripes in the warp, and more. Because she is the first to create many designs, she gets copied a lot—the sign of a trendsetter. Cortes are woven on foot looms, so a backstrap weaver must buy hers. With many to choose from, Lola has consistently insisted on wearing, even special ordering when necessary, the traditional deep red and jaspe corte of Atitlán that was the fashion from the 1930s to the 1960s, thus contributing to its return to popularity.

If a weaver is not careful to keep her baskets of yarn well separated, it is thought that the sprite from one will jump across and tangle the yarn in the other.

Lola's excitement about creativity is infectious, and our discussion of changes in fashion was fun, inspiring, and enlightening. Based on both the woven base cloth and the embroidery, with Lola's help we identified ten patterns of huipils and nine ways to decorate the neck. Because all are mixed and matched, it's nearly guaranteed that a woman would have a unique huipil. In addition to such variety in the overall look of both cloth and embroidery, the weft stripes woven in the local version of brocade use many different designs and yarns.

As with fashion trends anywhere, what's old may become new again and what's new passes away. Ironically, while Lola loves to use embroidery to express all the ideas in her head, it is the older style of nonembroidered huipil that she prefers. At least sometimes. So she joins the two, embroidering spectacular neck pieces to complement the woven-only body.

Although in the past she embroidered orchids and calla lilies, now birds are her favorite. As described earlier, Lola uses three distinct layouts of birds on huipils. Inside square frames created by colors in warp and weft, she embroiders both comical birds and realistic ones; some of her birds are flying within a row created by brocaded horizontal lines; others are flying all over her huipils. Possibly the most popular book in Santiago Atitlán is the Audubon bird book, from which many embroiderers have gotten not just their inspiration but factual information about the size, shape, and proportions of real birds. The artistry of Lola's birds includes all aspects: color, scale, design—and astonishing technique. It all adds up to stunning beauty, the reflection of a real artist.

Lola and Manuel are very active in their community, and their living room wall is covered with acknowledgements of civic contributions. One important project was not the kind that

earns a plaque but made a life-saving difference in the lives of a hundred families.

Atitlán is located on the southern shore of one of Guatemala's most beautiful attractions, Lake Atitlán, surrounded by the volcanoes San Pedro, Atitlán, and Tolimán. Many of the men of Atitlán have spent their lives working on the mountains behind the town where coffee farms, cacao beans, lumber cutting, and other agricultural pursuits keep them busy all year. That industry was severely curtailed during the *Conflicto Armado* (Armed Conflict). The 1980s were especially hard, and most men came down off the mountain in order to save their own lives. Confrontations between the guerrillas and the military were frequent, and anyone not in uniform was assumed to be either a guerrilla or a sympathizer. Either one made a man a target.

From 1983 to 1987, Manuel and Lola had a client in California who bought sashes from them. Designed by Lola, the sashes were 15 to 20 centimeters (6 to 8 inches) wide and woven by women on backstrap looms. At the peak, they were shipping 4,800 sashes per month. This work was a tremendous help for the families of the men who had to come down off the mountain. The project was a business, but it was also a community service.

Manuel completed sixth grade, but Lola completed only second grade; it was important to them that their children go further. Now, all three of their healthy children are school teachers—and artists. Sara Antonia is a beadworker, Allen Nicolás is a musician and calligrapher, and Jorge Manual draws. It is a point of pride that all have done so well. It is also a good connecting point for Lola and her school design work, because some of it comes from the school where her daughter teaches.

Just as Lola creates several styles of huipils, so Manuel's creativity leads him to paint in several styles. He showed us his way of preserving the culture through stories. His paintings show traditional life in its many forms, the day-to-day life in a pueblo. In those paintings, he records the clothing that was used in a particular time and place, providing a visual historical record.

Santiago Atitlán is one of the few communities where men still wear traditional dress. Usually white three-quarter-length pants with stripes of a darker color, such as maroon or purple, these daily-use pants do not have embroidery. When Manuel's daily-use pants wear out, Lola cuts them apart and reuses the cloth that is still in good condition to make small objects—frame-worthy art, coin purses, small pouches, and more. For festivals and special

Opposite: Volcan Santiago overlooking Lake Atitlán at dawn.

Below: Repairing any stripe of a backstrap warp is very difficult to do. Repairing a jaspe stripe is harder still. Lola says that she was careless and put her yarn baskets too close together—and now look!

occasions, the men wear pants that do have embroidery, and most men have birds flying around their legs from the hems up to their thighs. Because Lola loves to embroider and is always doing something new, she makes Manuel's birds smaller than most, which means there are more of them.

The most unique piece of traje in Atitlán is the *tocoyal*, a woman's head adornment. (There is no good English translation.) Although many communities have a special and unique way for a woman to wrap her head and/or her hair, Santiago Atitlán's is definitely the most dramatic. In fact, it's so impressive that a woman from Atitlán wearing a tocoyal is featured on Guatemla's 25c coin.

Called the Crown of the Princess, the tocoyal is about 2.5 centimeters (1 inch) wide and 16 meters (18 yards) long. The tocoyal is not premade and placed on the head like a hat. It is wrapped around and around every time it is put on. Most of it is red, with only the outer circle having other colors and designs, which also change with fashion. Lola first wore one when she was ten, but like most women in Atitlán she quit wearing it all the time. She now wears it only for special occasions, such as Semana Santa. Lola is a member of her church choir, and the women in the choir wear them when they perform.

We asked Lola what her work means to her, and what she would say to the textile artisans reading about her. She told us that to do the work requires concentration, and when she is focused, she lets go of everything else in the world.

If anyone wants to come and visit, she would be happy to welcome them as distinguished guests, share her work and ideas, and see their work and hear their ideas as well. Having special guests makes her feel important.

"God gave me a gift to be able to do many things. I don't have a formal education. My art is how people know me."

At top: A traditional tocoyal is not like a hat that is simply placed on the head. It is wrapped from beginning to end every time it is worn. If it gets knocked off in a crowd the wrapping begins again, and it's harder than it looks.

Above: Manuel Reanda and Lola Sapalú, artists together for forty years

IT'S ALL ABOUT CHOCOLATE AND COLOR

All conquerors are interested in the rich resources of their new lands. When the Spaniards arrived in Guatemala, they discovered a number of highly desirable plants, and quickly the King of Spain started demanding large quantities. In the 1500s, cacao—the base of chocolate—was at the top of the list.

Through the system of *encomiendas,* a combination of forced labor and heavy *tributos* (tributes/taxes), the local Maya population was told what they had to deliver. South of Lake Atitlán is an excellent cacao-growing area. In 1541, the town of Santiago Atitlán was founded; in 1543, just two years later, the taxable population of Atitlán had reached 1,000, bigger than most towns at that time. The town's tribute was 1,200 *xiquipiles* of cacao beans. One xiquipile equals 8,000 beans, which means that this community of 1,000 people was required to deliver 9,600,000 cacao beans that year.

Jump to the 1600s. From observing the indigenous population's use of color, the Spanish had discovered *jiquilite* (or *xiquilite*), the species of indigo that grew in Guatemala. They determined that jiquilite yields an especially strong and long-lasting blue color used for tomb-painting as well as textiles. When the King of Spain saw the superior quality of the indigo, he ordered a major increase in production for commercial purposes. Unfortunately, the conditions created by the process for extracting the indigo were highly toxic, and entire villages of workers died. The Spanish king ordered the cessation of the most damaging practices, and even sent visiting judges as monitors, but with limited effectiveness. During that century, indigo passed cacao as the biggest export crop.

Back in the 1500s, recognizing the great benefit that Mexico had in its production of *cochineal* (a small insect that lives on cactus and yields a red dye), the then-president of the region, Pedro de Villalobos, asked the king for permission to increase cochineal production, which would provide a means to expand and facilitate the tributes paid by the Maya. He got permission, but the project did not become a success. Nevertheless, the worldwide demand for cochineal continued, and in 1812, production was started anew. By 1825, cochineal was Guatemala's largest export. As of 2013, cacao is low on the export list, and indigo and cochineal are not on it at all. The largest export crop is now coffee, followed by sugar.

Photo: Howard Sandler/shutterstock.com

Chapter 5

ANTONIO RAMÍREZ SOSÓF

Santiago Atitlán, Sololá

Tz'utujil

Antonio Ramírez Sosóf, eighty-seven, was a lumberjack for thirty years. He often wore a green t-shirt to work until it became clear that to do so was dangerous. In the 1980s, the military had a detachment camped outside Santiago Atitlán. From that base they had many encounters with guerrillas and guerrilla sympathizers, and with others whom they accused of being one or the other. One way they identified those groups was by their clothing, which was often green. Antonio got the message: for your own safety, get off the mountain. So he did. He was then in his fifties.

At nearly ninety, *Don* Antonio is an internationally recognized embroidery artist. His works resemble paintings, except the medium is stitched thread. His subjects are stories, from many traditions: Tz'utujil life past and present, Bible stories, local legends, and historical events. Occasionally, he would stitch a duplicate if someone ordered one, but otherwise, each piece was unique. Unfortunately, those times are in the past. Because of a cataract surgery that went badly, Antonio is almost completely blind. That stops him from embroidering but not from continuing to sparkle.

In his early twenties, Antonio was married to Concepción Simac. They had six children, four of whom died. Then Concepción herself died, ending a twenty-year marriage and leaving Antonio with a son and a daughter. Two years later, he married Magdalena Quejú, and they had one son. After their twenty-year marriage, Magdalena also died. By then Antonio had come down off the mountain, so Magdalena had seen the remarkable transformation from lumberjack to artist.

Perhaps something about Atitlán's water creates artists. Not the water one drinks; instead, the famously beautiful Lake Atitlán, which would bring out the artist in anyone. Located on the south shore of the lake, the town of Atitlán is a veritable artists' colony. Painters of many styles, sculptors using fine or rustic wood, beaders working freeform or with looms, backstrap and foot-loom weavers, pen-decorators who use nylon cord or polymer clay, and embroiderers both traditional and modern. All these and more show their skill in the art market part of town. No one could fail to notice the arts; they're part of the atmosphere. So when many men had to come down from the mountain, it's not surprising that some of them turned to the arts.

Having worked with wood for more than thirty years, Antonio's first artistic endeavor was wood carving, working with roots

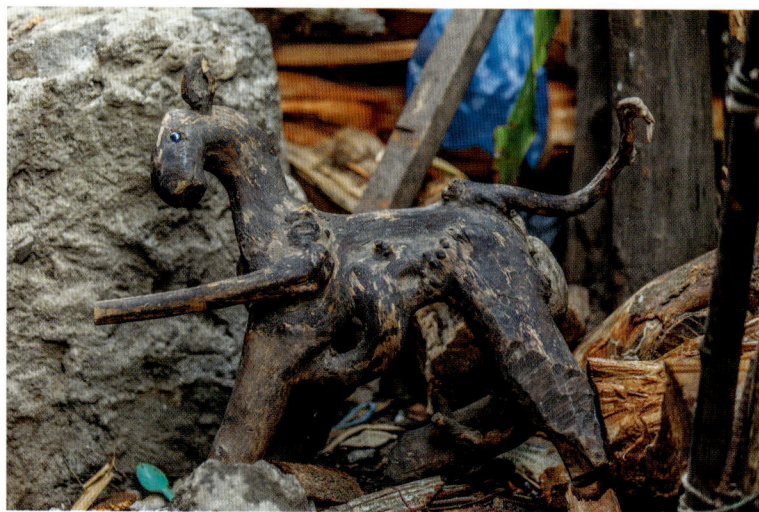

Above: Antonio's first venture into the world of art led him to carving tree roots and branches into the characters that were already there. He quickly developed an international following—and shoulder problems.

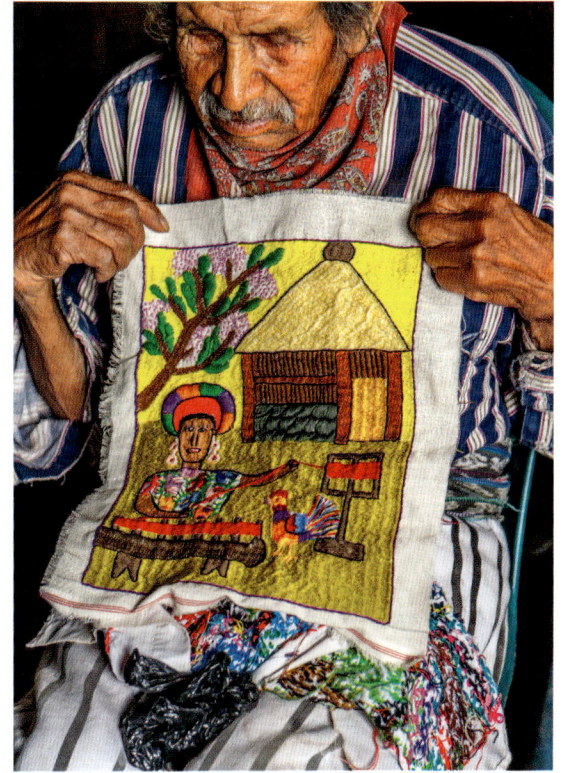

and branches of the trees he knew so well. He let the shape of the wood tell him what it was to be, and the result was a folk art that attracted foreign attention as well as local. However, the physical effort of the carving took a toll on Antonio's back and shoulders, so he had to give it up.

One night he had a dream that gave him the idea for the rest of his life's work as an artist. In the dream, he saw a portrait, but it was not a painting. It was an embroidery of a woman wearing an embroidered huipil. He was surprised, and intrigued. He thought embroidery was something he could do even though he knew nothing about it. And so Antonio began the process of teaching himself—about needles, yarns, backings, color, design, subject matter. In the end, he had been right; he could do it.

The most frequent question he has been asked is "Where do you get the ideas for your work?" His most frequent answer has been "From divine inspiration, from God." Sometimes God has spoken to him through other people asking him about stories, for example in a Tz'utujil community, how do a boy and girl flirt and become boyfriend and girlfriend? In the *temascal* (Maya sauna), is one clothed or naked? Those questions and others gave him the idea to show scenes from the traditional life of the Tz'utujil. His connection to trees led him to create a picture of a pair of trees that are clearly male and female. "You have to have both to make new trees," he tells us, smiling. He has done so many pieces over the course of the last twenty years that now he has albums full of pictures of his pieces, many of which are hanging in other countries.

Antonio himself has none of his own pieces, but a dozen or so are hanging at the *Posada de Santiago*, a beautiful stone-built inn for people looking for a comfortably elegant get-away. First, Susie Gunn Glanville and later David Glanville—both of whom are great fans of his work—helped Antonio with promotion both pre- and post-Internet. With their help, he has shipped his embroideries to many countries. He has been told that he is a registered artist in both Guatemala and Spain, but he does not know if it's true. Some Mexican musicians said they would write a song about him; he does not know if they ever did.

As Antonio has aged, and even more, as he knew he was losing his sight, he did not want his art to die with him. His

Right: Now on permanent display at the Posada de Santiago, Antonio's embroideries have been inspired by the two traditions he knows best, the life and legends of the Tz'utujil and Christianity.

Below top: In a world where adequate medical care is non-existent for many, the promise of the healing power of Jesus inspires hope.

Below bottom: Antonio and part of his family.

grandson Pedro Pop became his student, and the two of them embarked on the teaching/learning journey that Antonio never really had. Draw designs on the cloth first. This yarn behaves in this way, this other one in a different way. Needles—why use a particular one? Color—which colors go well together, which don't? Subjects—Antonio found his; Pedro will find his own. Although Pedro has clients, including in the United States, he does not have enough embroidery work to support his family, so he still works as a *jornalero* (day laborer). But Antonio's art will go on. And watching the life of his grandfather has surely taught Pedro that career changes can sometimes be quite surprising.

As is normal for the oldest generation, Antonio is now living with his three children, rotating among them week by week. As we wind our way through the honeycombed architecture common to the area, visiting him is a painful reminder that fame does not equal fortune. And yet his spirit and mind are both fully intact and the enthusiasm that emanates from Antonio can only elicit smiles from his visitors. Perhaps because he cannot see well enough to retrieve his things easily and because he is a thin man wearing a large shirt, all of the things he wanted to show us were within reach—in bags tucked inside his shirt. The fact that he could not see each bag did not matter. With a craftsman's touch, he could feel from the outside what each bag contained, opening the right one as its part in the conversation came up. In a similar way, his large bandana was his bank, each knotted area holding a separate "account," for example money from pieces sold or money for medicine. On our last visit, the surrounding family members, mostly from the generation of grandchildren, were enjoying the conversation as much as we were. While Antonio came from a pre-electricity life that prepared him to be a lumberjack, one of his granddaughters was happy to give us her email address. He was her age in 1950, worlds apart from 2014. And yet his art won't die, and that has value in any generation.

Chapter 6

EMILIA CHAY POZ

Zunil, Quetzaltenango
K'iche'

Emilia Chay Poz, fifty-nine, shines with joy and inspires it in those around her. She has had hard times and good times; neither defines her. She is simply a woman who can look back on her life and say, "I'm content. It has not been an easy life. We had a rough start. But now it's okay."

As a little girl, Emilia looked forward to starting school; she could hardly wait. Finally, her father took her to enroll, a memorable day. The next day, he abandoned the family for another woman, and Emilia's school career was over. Instead, she helped support the family of her mother and two sisters. "I would go to work in the vegetable fields at 3 a.m. and work until mid-day. Then, I would come home and do household chores until 7 p.m. I earned pennies. There were days that we did not have food to eat."

In 1960, a German priest, Father Siegfried Fleiner, arrived in Zunil. An entrepreneur at heart, he noticed many marketable skills in the town that could be used to help people increase their income to more than "pennies." In textiles in particular, he saw a town full of excellent backstrap weavers weaving only for their own use, not selling anything, yet these same weavers bought their *cintas* (hair ribbons) from Totonicapan instead of weaving and selling them themselves. It seemed obvious that they should weave their own cintas. It was obvious, but not easy.

Changing from weaving warp-faced huipils on a backstrap loom to weaving weft-faced cintas on a foot loom requires not only a totally different use of the body, but an equally significant conceptual shift as well. Nevertheless, a few young women were willing to take on the challenge. At age fourteen, Emilia was one of them. She liked learning new things. This is Emilia's memory of that time.

"The women who decided to learn," she said, "were taken to Totonicapan by our missionary friend Pablo to ask the cinta weavers to teach us. The response was a clear no. 'If you weave your own cintas, you will take away our *tamalitos* and our *atol*.' Not only did the cinta weavers refuse to teach us, they threatened us with violence if we persisted in trying to learn." (*Tamalitos*—in this area, a fit-in-your-hand-sized loaf of corn masa eaten instead of tortillas; *atol*—a hot corn-based drink.)

Emilia told us that eventually Pablo made contact with Father Tomás Garcia in San Andres Xecul, near Toto. He knew a weaver, Andrea Garcia, whose daughter Marina was willing to move to Zunil to teach the women to weave cinta. Marina was sixteen. She stayed in Zunil for six months, long enough for thirteen women (of the twenty-seven who started) to become proficient enough to teach others. Within three years, most of the cinta weaving for Zunil was being done in Zunil.

Although in Atitlán, the drama is in how the cinta (see page 40) is worn, in Zunil, the drama is in the cinta itself. So what is so dramatic and so challenging that it took six months to learn?

Of all the textiles represented in this book, the cintas of Zunil are the smallest and among the most intense. At 2.5 centimeters (1 inch) wide and 2.77 meters (3 yards) long, they have 18 warp threads and an uncountable number of weft threads. Woven as tiny tapestries, they traditionally had a rainbow of colors that created tiny images of men and women, rabbits, and a fantastic assortment of geometric shapes. Some have designs the entire length of the cinta; others have a solid-colored center section. They all have handmade pom-poms at both ends.

The cinta is woven with a mix of structures, all weft faced. Watching Emilia weave and unable to determine what made her

switch from one to the other, I finally asked, "How do you decide when to change?" She answered, "When the cinta asks for it." Of course.

The loom, which has not changed in more than a hundred years, is part counterbalanced, part backstrap, part "other." Materials have changed as new ones have become available. Over the years, the warp has been a strong white cotton sized with watered-down carpenters' glue. The weft has been cotton (unmercerized until there was mercerized), silk, acrylic, or rayon of various kinds. The

Circa 1970, the cinta loom Emilia is working on launched a new industry and provided a step toward textile independence in the area of Zunil. It was a dangerous tool of subversive thoughts and actions.

The cinta loom is a hybrid of several others. A four-shaft loom with only two treadles, shaft one is tied to the left treadle, shaft three to the right treadle. Shafts two and four have heavy weights attached to their lams, which pull those shafts down when allowed to. So, stepping down on the left treadle lifts the weighted/heavier shaft (#2 up so #1 down); letting go of the treadle allows the weighted shaft to drop down (#2 down, #1 up). The warp is extended forward from the loom out and around a distant anchor and forms a loop that is tied to Emilia's waist—note maroon belt around her waist on this page and the next. As she weaves she rotates the loop around, and as she does there is less blank warp in front of her and more woven cinta on her right. Her body provides the tension to make the warp tight enough to weave. The heddles on this loom are also very clever. A polypropylene rope is slightly untwisted, a grommet inserted, and then the rope twists back, holding the grommet in place. Instant smooth and large-eyed heddles!

Emilia is wearing modern traje, the latest style that still has shades of earlier Zunil styles. Her huipil is made with two panels woven with warp stripes and no other patterning. They are sewn together in the middle on a home sewing machine, making a wide and colorful *randa*. Sewing machines often have both electric motors and treadles so they can be used with or without electricity.

Emilia's corte was woven on a foot loom, each row of each flower picked up by the weaver's fingers. Small skeins of colored weft, called butterflies, are used to fill in the designs. The black background weft is carried on a boat shuttle. The corte is worn with the warp running not from hem to waist but around the weaver; the selvedges are at her waist and hem. To make the corte wide enough, that is, long enough to go below her knees, two pieces are joined. Just below her maroon belt you can see a smaller randa, hand-embroidered.

Now eighty-three years old, Emilia's mother Ventura grew up wearing cinta woven in Totonicapan. Thanks first to curiosity and later to the courage of Emilia and her friends, Ventura now wears cinta woven in Zunil.

pom-poms are made of the same yarn as the weft. The weaver makes the pom-poms, and also leaves foot-long tails hanging, usually of all the colors used. It takes ten to fifteen days to weave one cinta, and at present they sell in the co-op that Emilia is part of for Q. 300 (about $39). (Used ones are available for less.)

As with all things related to clothing, fashions change. The biggest threat to the Zunil cinta is that younger women are choosing not to wear them. But for those who do, there are changes in color (monochromatics are popular now) and in design (fruits and flowers are in fashion).

The Santa Ana cooperative was started in 1968 and the cinta weaving project was one of its earliest endeavors. It would not be possible to tell Emilia's story without telling some of the co-op's story as well.

Starting in buildings belonging to the parish, the cooperative had the support of a group of German and Austrian Catholics living in Zunil. In particular, Annie Weirmeyer de Wagner helped start the co-op both legally and functionally. From the beginning, the co-op established a self-governing plan that included an administrator, office jobs, committee heads, and everyone on down to the membership at large. Some were paid positions, some volunteer. In addition to helping the co-op get established, the Catholic community also facilitated sales of the weaving in Europe, an economic assist that gave the co-op a reason to exist. In time, again with the help of friends, the coop moved into its own building, where it still is.

As sales have risen and fallen over the years, the cooperative has needed to expand its services. Foreseeing that from the start, the full legal name of the cooperative is The Santa Ana Cooperative of Weavers and Diverse Services, Ltd. In addition to the retail textile store, the co-op has a school supply store, a yarn store for members, classroom and meeting room space, and offices. They also receive *remesas* (money coming from family in the United States) and offer microcredit to members. (Another benefit is the back patio, which has a drop-dead gorgeous view overlooking Zunil's onion fields and the rugged mountains just beyond.)

A member from the beginning, Emilia has always thought of the co-op as her second home. She took on a range of volunteer leadership roles in her first twenty years and has been an employee now for more than twenty years. When she was in a leadership role, she experienced the most frightening time of her life.

During the Time of the Violence, many men in the community of La Estancia de la Cruz, down the mountain from Zunil, were killed, leaving widows and orphans behind. Some of these women learned to sew and became members of the co-op. "How did that time affect Zunil itself?" we asked.

"It was very bad here," Emilia and her husband Pedro answered together. "The judiciales were here looking for people, anyone who had a leadership position in any group, even the cooperative. Some neighbors came and said that the judiciales had come and shown them a picture of Emilia and asked where she lived because they were going to kill her. They had pictures of other people who were leaders too, and asked people where they lived because they were going to kill them for being guerrillas," they told us. "The priest who had helped us had to run away in the middle of the night and go to Mexico to hide. We took our four children and went to hide in the home of Emilia's sister. Her house is away from the main road, so you would only see it if you knew to look for it. We lived there for a year."

"Things began to calm down by 1988," they continued. "The judiciales captured a woman who was a guerrilla but did not kill her because she was pregnant. They showed her the list they had and she told them who really was a guerrilla and who was not. Lots of people got put on the list just because someone who did not like them told the soldiers that they were guerrillas. She told them that Emilia and many others were not guerrillas, and after that we could go back home."

Emilia grew up as the middle of three sisters. Her mother did not own any land, so they always worked as day laborers for others who did. As an adult, Emilia's mother received Q. 15 ($2) per month. As a child, if Emilia harvested, bundled, and carried Swiss chard to the market, she was paid 5 cents a day (½ cent U.S.). If she only harvested them, she received 3 cents.

When she was fifteen, Emilia married Pedro Quixtan Poz, and as is the custom (still), moved in with him and his parents. The couple lived there for six months before moving into their own home. Over the years, they were able to buy some land of

Zunil is built on steep hillsides dropping down to the Samala River. Many houses look at their neighbors up or down instead of side to side. The corn that has been harvested is now drying on the roof in preparation for knocking it off the cobs (by thumb) to be stored for future use making tortillas.

their own, where they grew onions—the primary crop of Zunil—and other vegetables. Pedro had made it through sixth grade, and though Emilia never got back to school, she did take two years of literacy classes as an adult so she can read and sign her name. Now, their daughter is in the university, studying to be a dentist; she wears traje but not cinta. Their three sons are all working in the United States. Emilia and Pedro are sad that they have not seen them in almost fifteen years, but they are happy that they can know their granddaughter via the Internet. Emilia was in the United States on an Economic Development trip in the early 1990s. They had hoped to get another visa that would allow them to visit their sons, but they were turned down. Meanwhile, they are grateful for the money that their sons have been able to send back; it has allowed them to build a comfortable concrete-block home in front of the smaller adobe home they had lived in since they came out of hiding.

Being with Emilia and Pedro is a pleasure. Pedro, a strong and supportive man, quietly helps Emilia with her various health problems. His love for her is reflected back in hers for him. They've had more than forty challenging years together, so it is no small thing when she says, "I'm content."

CORTES—MAYA WOMEN'S SKIRTS

Most of the time, huipils get all the attention, and with good reason. They are spectacular, and no one will ever see them all. But the lowly corte has a lot of variety, too, and beauty of its own.

Adult cortes are 8 varas in length. A vara is an old Spanish measurement equal to 84 centimeters (33.6 inches), so 8 varas equals 6.72 meters (7.47 yards) of fabric in one corte. Why so long? It handles cold weather, can be rotated for cleanliness and wear, and will fit when a woman is pregnant as easily as when she is not.

How it is worn, how it is fastened, how long it lasts—all these are part of the story, but it is the cloth itself that calls for attention. Describing five cortes (a nonscientific yet representative sample) will give you an idea of the variety that exists.

Without a doubt, the jaspes of Salcajá are the winners in terms of quantity. Sold all over the country, various regions have color preferences, and hotter places prefer double jaspe (jaspe in both warp and weft) because it's a lighter-weight fabric. Within the Salcajá jaspe category, you can always find a new style to enjoy, as well as an almost infinite number of choices. (A fuller explanation of Salcajá jaspe follows on page 58.)

Chichicastenango also has a jaspe corte, but it's a totally different style of jaspe—bolder, weft jaspe only. The Chichi corte is pieced together with a *randa*, a seam completely hidden by striking embroidery that is a major part of its decoration. Chichi cortes tend to be worn shorter than in most places.

In Nahualá, the corte is nearly solid navy blue. Originally indigo, the blue is now called morga. The corte has a few thin stripes, mostly white, but sometimes fancier, sometimes with even a stripe of dark jaspe. This corte also has a randa, though not as bold as the Chichi randa. It is finer and has more embroidered designs, ranging from flowers to water bottles.

Santa Catarina Palopó's corte is mostly turquoise, like the area's huipil; both are cloth expressions of the turquoise of Lake Atitlán. What stands out in Santa Catarina's corte, which is woven with weft-faced stripes, is the sparkle. Like the diamonds twinkling on the water of the lake, metallic threads create sparkles in the corte.

The corte of Almolonga, Quetzaltenango, has narrow ⅓ twill stripes in it. It is woven in such soft colors that the twill is only visible from a very short distance. But it's worth looking for because in those stripes, the back and front show up as different colors. A semi-secret delight.

Other unique cortes abound—Zunil, Colotenango, Rabinal, the Ixil Triangle, and more. But for every town that has its own corte, probably ten wear cortes from Salcajá or its neighbors. The jaspe corte of Salcajá truly does reign.

Chapter 7

JUAN DE DIOS RODAS GÁLVEZ
Salcajá, Quetzaltenango
Ladino
Spanish

"Weaving is dignified work. There are old men who need work. I give them the simplest jobs, just so they can have something to do. Work is a tool against poverty, and one's state of mind is as important for survival as money."

—Juan de Dios Rodas Gálvez

I s Juan de Dios, fifty, a compassionate man with a good handle on business or an administrator with a social conscience and a loom? Clearly, he is both. He wanted to go to college to study economics but chose to support his family as the more responsible alternative. However, that did not stop him from learning, and listening to him is like having a crash course in business administration, with real live examples for every lesson. Because of his experience and knowledge, we have included some passages from our conversation throughout his story.

… …

The work of artisans is not respected, and it should be. But the artisans need to give that respect also. They need to treat their work like a real job, with set hours, doing quality work always. We formed a group to sell to a client in Holland. The client was very clear that quality was critical, as were the deadlines, and everyone in the group assured him that they would produce only the best and send it on time. They didn't do either one, so that was that. The client never ordered again, and the group dissolved. People want steady work that comes fast. They don't want the demands, delays, and expenses of exporting. The market in Europe and the United States is not the same as here. Here, a corte is a necessity; there it is a decoration. That requires a different approach.

Juan's father was a jaspe weaver, as was his grandfather. He doesn't know any further back than that. His own father wove until he was about ninety-five, and lived to be more than one hundred. If his grandfather wove until he was seventy-five, then, when Juan is included, the family has been weaving jaspe for more than two centuries.

Juan began in his father's workshop at the same time he started first grade, when he was eight years old. Juan was the youngest of four brothers; the other three were weaving as well. His father had only one loom, so as they got old enough, each son went to work in another workshop. Eventually, Juan worked for one of his brothers. When he was eighteen he rejoined his father, and they switched roles.

… …

Smart business is essential, and enough. Keep regular hours (6 a.m. to 4 p.m.). Be efficient with equipment. Small adjustments lead to big savings: use two feet to treadle instead of one; move the beater 1.3 centimeters (½ inch) up or down to hit the cloth more effectively. Pay attention to the thickness of the roller that the shafts hang from because if it has too small a circumference the shafts will be too close together and will rub against each other and slow down the weaving.

Within six months, Juan-the-business-administrator had brought in another loom. Later, he added more. Over the years, there have been more during boom times, fewer in the slower times. Right now, Juan has two looms in his own workshop and five more in the community, with weavers who weave for him in their homes.

… …

What can happen to weavers is that out of a need for cash, they sell their work for what it cost them to make it or even a little less. That gives them money for food tonight, but then they don't have enough to buy raw materials for their next cloth. So they make less cloth, then sell it for too little again, then they can only make less.

But the workshop weavers don't work "for him"; that is not the right terminology, as he makes clear. He is not an owner or a boss, but an administrator, coordinating the work of about thirty to thirty-five people performing different steps in the jaspe process. If Juan is not present, his wife, Eufemia, does the job. Among them all, they can produce fifteen cortes per week, enough to

Juan de Dios in the workshop he grew up in. He knows that both his father and his grandfather wove jaspe. He doesn't know for sure if his great-grandfather did.

Some of the steps involved in making jaspe. Juan's daughter taking off the tight wrappings that make the jaspe. Each white section is where the warp was wrapped prior to dying. Weft—winding a dozen skeins for tying and dyeing, each will fill one bobbin. Warp—measuring warp on a room-sized warping mill.

Opposite: Jaspe: dyed (black), untied (black and white), and wound on bobbins ready to weave.

keep everyone working. Juan is very proud of the fact that he can perform all the steps involved, and loves to. So if someone cannot work at a given time, he can fill in and do his or her job. He reserves three steps for himself all of the time, the three that are most critical to quality control*. However, he is happy doing any and all of them as needed. (See page 58.)

One of Juan's staunchest beliefs, which he expresses repeatedly in a number of ways, is the value of stability over the vicis-

situdes of fashion. Most outsiders don't see the changes in corte, but in fact style changes are constant—in color, design, complexity, fibers and yarns, not to mention regional preferences. Even dye methods change. As with fashion anywhere, the demand goes up and down. Up means more work; down means laying people off, something Juan is loath to do. So he has half a dozen or so designs that are his stock in trade, and with those, a constant eye on efficiency, and an ongoing search for markets, he has managed to keep his workshop going for thirty years.

…… ……

If I change designs, then I have to change weavers. Each one knows how to do one thing, and to learn something new would take time. I don't want to have to let people go.

What does that mean in terms of stability in his own life? Juan loves the work, is profoundly impressed with the dignity and decency of it while just plain enjoying the hands-on aspects. But even more important is what it has allowed him in terms of family life. Being an artisan has meant he could work at home, be there as his three daughters were growing up. Juan relates that in Salcajá, from which many people have emigrated to the United States, broken homes are all too prevalent. There are single mothers for the usual reasons of divorce and abandonment, but many are because the men have gone north. Among other things, that means a lot of kids left on their own much of the time, without jobs or healthy activities, and too many end up as gang members. Even if their dads come back, if they can't find jobs, it's still a tough situation.

…… ……

The price of yarn and dyes has gone way up, the demand for cortes has gone way down, and the number of weavers has increased, so the competition is greater than ever. Many of the agricultural jobs that used to support so many families have also disappeared. People used to go to the coast to harvest cotton and sugar. Now cotton is gone and employment in the sugar fields has decreased.

Even at its best, the world of jaspe cortes has been hard from a numbers standpoint, as evidenced by all of Juan's brothers choosing other careers. Juan thought about going to the United States too, but for the sake of both his family and the people who work with him, he decided it would be better to stay. He is happy with what the work has afforded him, but he wants his daughters to have better options. So he worked hard to be sure they did, and now two have college degrees, and one is still studying. Unfortunately, there are still no jobs, so his two older daughters with college degrees are now starting families in the United States and doing whatever jobs they can find without legal papers. "Even a low-paying job in the United States is better than no job at all in Guatemala," he says.

About our visit, Juan was very pleased that someone was interested enough to really understand the process. In part, educating people about jaspe could help in the sale of jaspe cortes outside of Guatemala, and in part, he is just really excited about new knowledge—anyone learning anything. Juan's father never went to school, so though he made sure that his sons did, he also taught them his own curriculum. Their "school of life" included the fundamentals: responsibility, honesty, honor, integrity, and striving for quality in everything.

With his daughters moving on to better opportunities, what does that mean for the future of Juan's jaspe workshop? "I value weaving jaspe for the work, and I also love it. I love tying the designs, I love weaving. It's a good life," he says. "But when I die, my workshop will die also. That's the reality of the future, and it's okay. I'm not sad. I did the job I had to do on the planet."

JASPE—THE STEPS INVOLVED

Jaspe (pronounced HA-spay) is the Guatemalan form of ikat (pronounced EE-cot), an ancient and admired art form found in a number of other cultures. It is basically tie-dye done on yarn before the yarn is woven, so the designs created by the tied areas show up in the finished cloth. The jaspe process is hugely complex and time-consuming.

The word jaspe can refer to either the final cloth or the process used to create that cloth. The process takes many steps, which are performed by a team of people. Although the process could be handled by just one or two people, in Guatemala jaspe is all about production, and specialization works better for everyone.

Jaspe is a method of creating designs while weaving a plain-weave cloth. The cloth can be warp-faced for vertical designs, weft-faced for horizontal designs, or a balanced weave for double jaspe, with the designs crossing each other as they go in both directions. But in all cases, it has a plain-weave structure. Warp jaspe is more difficult to set up and easier to weave; weft jaspe is easier to set up and more difficult to weave. And double jaspe is hard both to set up and weave. ("Easier" is relative.)

For you to appreciate the work and the lives of Juan de Dios Rodas (see page 54) and Tomasa Siquina (see page 62), the following list details the steps involved for warp jaspe, the more complex labor (jaspe with figures). Keep in mind that this process will create a stripe in the warp of between 1.9 centimeters (¾ inch) and 5 centimeters (2 inches) wide, depending on the pattern.

Wind 40 spools with .23 kilograms (8 ounces) of 20/2 cotton each.

*Wind the warp on a very large warping mill, twenty-seven revolutions to make twenty cortes, approximately 134 meters (146 yards).

Deliver the warp chain to the amarrador for tying the design.

Extend the warp full length, anywhere one can find a stretch of open space long enough. That might be beside the river, along the road, or on the side of a street in town. One of the amazing sights of Salcaja is seeing these warps stretched out everywhere.

Using a kind of multiple-tiered raddle (a sort of comb for keeping the threads organized), lay the warp into it by sections according to what the pattern calls for.

Double the warp back on itself, then double it again to make each section thicker.

Tie the pattern in, making the ties (or wrappings) where you don't want the dye to penetrate.

Contain the yarn gently to take it to the dye house.

Pre-soak the yarn in hot water, done in a large tub (the soaking is performed by a man wearing rubber boots).

Dye in hotter water, then squeeze out the excess.

Rinse as many times as needed. Hang to dry.

Pack up the yarn to return to the amarrador.

Stretch it out to its quadrupled length, taking the quadrupling ties off.

Put the three-tiered raddle in place, dividing the threads again.

Untie the first ten yards of resist wrappings.

Using the raddle, realign all the threads to create the pattern.

Untie all of the wrapping ties. (This job is a good one for kids, the first job many have.)

Moving the raddle along to align the pattern, tie new ties every couple of yards to hold the pattern in place.

Dip the warp into a sizing bath made of a starchy vegetable juice; let it dry.

*The warp designer determines where each stripe of jaspe and solid color will go to create a (.91 meter) 1-yard wide warp.

*Wind the warp onto the warp beam. (A four-person team with a hand-held raddle performs this task.)

Tie new warp to old warp behind the heddles, one thread at a time.

Pull the new warp through the heddles and reed and adjust the tension to be ready to weave.

Behind the heddles, untie the first row of pattern anchor ties to allow threads to pass through heddles. These are untied only as they approach the heddles.

Weave.

Juan de Dios says that it takes his team two weeks to get a jaspe warp onto the loom.

That's warp jaspe. Weft jaspe works on the same principle and would take an equally long explanation.

THE DYE HOUSE

It goes without saying that the dyeing of jaspe is fifty percent of what makes it jaspe. Over the centuries the methods have probably been pretty consistent, but advances in technology have made a difference: from clay pots to iron pots to sturdy plastic tubs; natural dyes to aniline dyes; tying and untying and re-tying for every color wanted in a multicolored warp to tying once and using a plastic syringe to change colors.

This is a family run dye house with a few non-family members, six or seven workers in total. They can dye 500 pounds dry weight in a day, for which they receive Q. 3 ($ .36)/lb., so a full-order day will pay Q. 1,500 (almost $200). Not every day is full, but they have steady clients so there is always some dyeing to do.

When they have finished their work the dyed yarns go back to the amarradora or amarrador to begin the process of untying all those knots and realigning the threads to create the images.

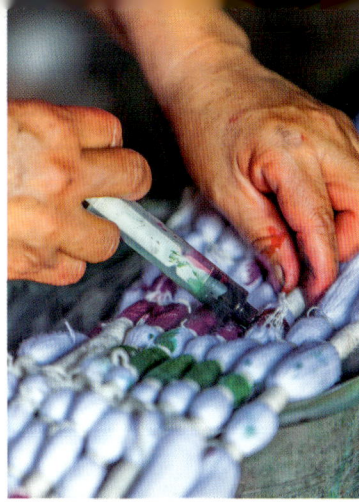

Opposite: The dye house.

This page top row: A mountain of warp waiting to be dyed black. When finished the now-white bundles will have a black background and white patterns. The multicolored bundles will have a black background and designs in all the colors now visible.

A relatively new more efficient way of making a multicolored jaspe stripe. Using a syringe, the dye of choice is injected under the resist ties. The black that comes later will dye the exposed sections but will not penetrate the tightly wrapped areas, so in the end the color injected will be the color of the design.

Middle row: Presoaking the threads helps the dye to be absorbed better.

Bottom row: Lifting a bundle of weft out of the dyepot. Ready to go back to the amarrador for untying all of those tightly wrapped sections. Different-sized sections create the patterns. The light dusting of brown on the right side has rubbed off the adobe wall behind the yarn and will rinse right off.

Chapter 8

Bacilia Tomasa Siquina Chanchavac
Salcajá, Quetzaltenango
K'iche'

I n Guatemala, many jobs in weaving are gender-specific, with men doing one thing and women another. Such is not the case with being an *amarrador,* a person who ties jaspe. Anyone with sufficient manual dexterity may do it, regardless of gender or age. Many steps are involved in creating jaspe cloth—arranging the threads, tying them with the design, then, after dyeing, realigning the threads. Those three steps determine how clearly the pictures in the cloth will show up. Tomasa, sixty-seven, is a highly skilled amarradora.

She is fortunate to have a perfect place to stretch out her warps. Eastern exposure for morning sun is good on cold mornings. The space is bordered by a row of cypress trees for shade once the day warms up. It is on grass, better for feet and legs than pavement, and what traffic there is doesn't disturb her. The 554-meter (600-yard) roadside stretch, shared with other jaspe tiers, is also close to her home, another plus. In the dry season, jaspe tiers work every day. In the rainy season, most mornings are clear but whether or not to work is an hourly decision.

Tomasa shared a story with us. "One day I was here tying jaspe. I had not one cent, nothing with which to buy food for my children. I had done some work for Clemente [Ruiz], and that day he came by and paid me. It was a miracle." She told us that when people stop by to see her work, she is happy to talk with them. When we approached her about being part of this project, she said yes, adding that though she is friendly with people who come to see her work, she does not invite them into her home. In our case, we were welcome—because I had been with Clemente that day. For her to share the story that follows required that level of trust.

Learning to tie jaspe didn't come easily for Tomasa. Her father was a jaspe tier, as was her grandfather. They mostly tied weft jaspe, and one of her jobs as a child was to prepare the threads for the tying. Her father, however, was abusive to both Tomasa and her mother, and he never taught her more than how to prepare the yarn. She then married a warp jaspe tier who was an alcoholic and who beat her regularly, especially while he was teaching her to tie jaspe. (Eventually, she left him.) "I suffered a lot for this work, but I thank God that he blessed me with it. With what I earned, I raised three daughters and helped two more."

Though she married at fourteen, Tomasa did not have her first daughter, Olga, until she was twenty-five. Her second daughter, Sara, was born when Tomasa was thirty-three. Then, she and her husband adopted a third daughter, whose daughter Sarita now lives with Tomasa in a three-room house that they share with Tomasa's parents, who are in their eighties. And, while they are building their own house, Olga and her second husband, who is a jaspe weaver, live there as well.

When Tomasa was old enough, she told her father that she wanted to go to school and he agreed. She enrolled and started attending. Then, according to Tomasa, "Someone said they were giving away a baby, and my mother said to my father that she was going to bring the baby [home]. My father agreed because my mother could not have any more children, and she went to bring it. Then they told me that I couldn't study because I had to take care of [the baby]. I told them I would study and they responded that I was not going to. I only studied seven months, and I did not go to study [anymore]. I took care of my brother and worked afterward. Time passed and I got married, and my husband taught me the work."

Tomasa and her daughter Olga beside the adobe house they both grew up in.

With the warp already dyed, Tomasa now ties the knots that keep the pattern in place. Depending on the complexity of the design, she can tie approximately 200 yards of warp per day.

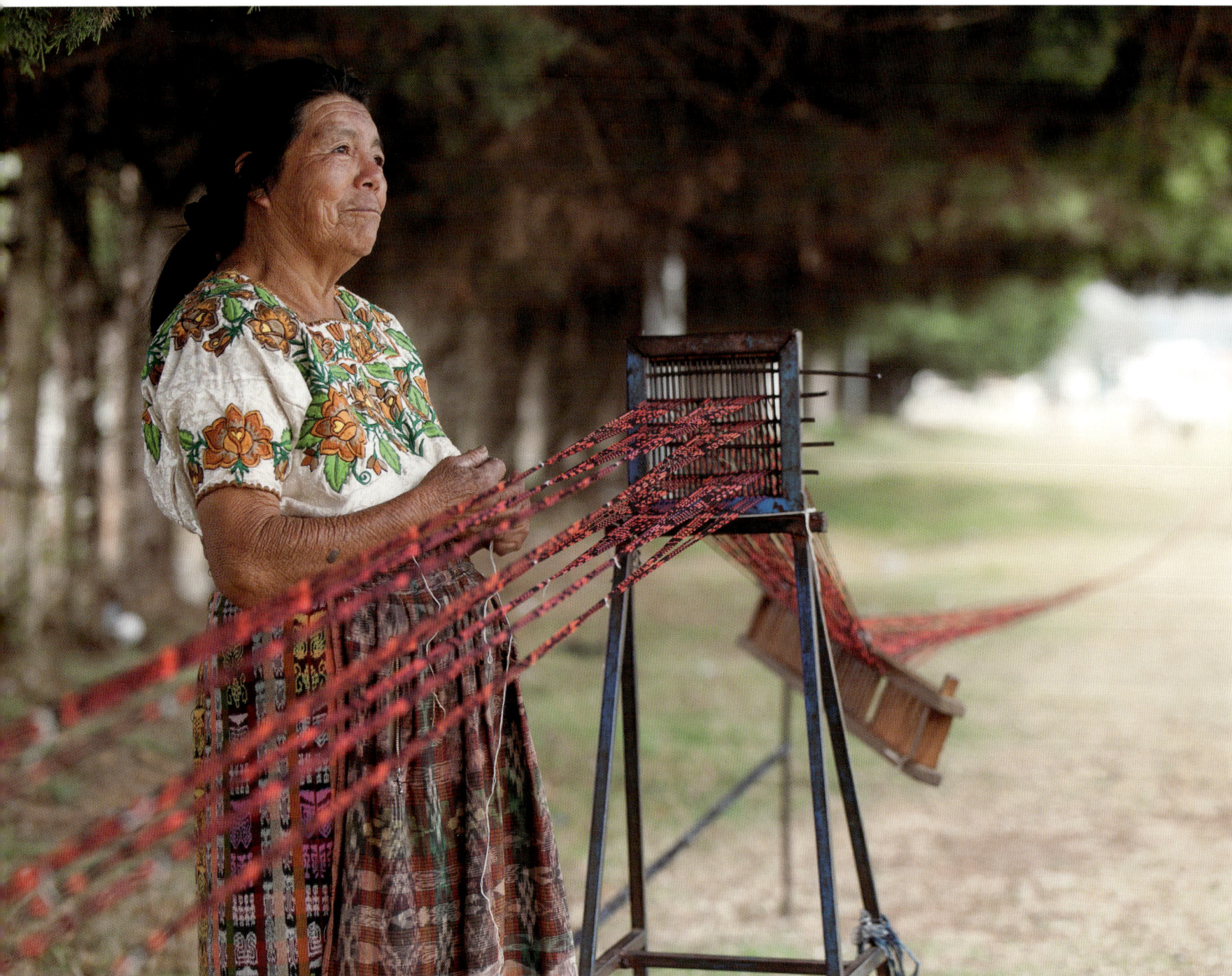

A jaspe warp rolled onto the warp beam of a loom. The small white wrappings near the bottom are what Tomasa is tying on to keep the jaspe motifs lined up.

Tomasa's own daughters finished sixth grade; Sarita is in junior high and likes school. She intends to keep studying to be a bookkeeper/accountant. Appreciating the value of the work, Tomasa taught all her girls how to be amarradoras. As an adult, Sara works with them sometimes, and for Olga it is a full-time job. Sarita helps her grandmother when she is not in school, to compensate for Tomasa's diminished eyesight.

A discussion of Guatemalan jaspe must note the difference between two styles, the simple and the complex. The simple style is called *jaspe.* In this style, the resist ties are all evenly spaced, so dividing and realigning are not necessary. The more complex style is called *labor.* In this style, the threads are divided into groups that eventually lead to images: water jars, men and women, corn plants, butterflies, flowers, and more than one hundred additional designs. The complexity of the design determines whether it will require more or fewer *cordeles* (cords), groups of threads tied and dyed together. Labor designs are mostly mirror images, so a pattern will require from five to fifteen cordeles, usually an odd number that gives an indication of the width of the design. More cordeles are needed for wider designs.

Tomasa told us that in the job she was working on, the patterns required five or seven cordeles. For example, it takes a minimum of five to do men, women, or leaves, and seven to do images of jars. When there is a new design, she gets a written diagram to follow. Some new patterns come from amarradores, others from the *patron*, the man who gives her work.

Tomasa has one patron, and, although the work is generally steady, there are times when he wants more than she can do and times when she doesn't have enough work. Olga has seven or eight patrons, but even so she gets fewer orders than Tomasa. No matter, the family works together to do the most work possible. The warps Tomasa receives will weave twenty-two cortes of eight varas each. Each vara is 84 centimeters (33.6 inches), so a warp would be longer than 138 meters (150 yards). She receives Q. 25 ($3.25) per labor and can do two a day (with Sarita's help), giving her an income of Q. 200 to Q. 300 (about $26 to $39) per week.

Despite all the difficulties in her life, Tomasa has a ready smile and a cheerful way about her. We asked her what she thought of our visit and our project. She answered, "It makes me happy because it recognizes me as an artist." And that made us happy.

"I thank God that he blessed me with this work. With what I earned I raised three daughters and helped two others."

SALCAJÁ— MECCA FOR WEAVERS

Salcajá has more weaving supplies for sale than likely the entire rest of the country combined. Dozens of little stores are mixed in with a few big ones and one really big one. They sell yarn—mostly cotton, rayon, and acrylic—in quantities ranging from an ounce to many pounds, principally for weaving or embroidery. A woman embroidering a huipil might buy a few skeins of floss in various colors while a man weaving jaspe cortes might buy as many hundreds of pounds of white cotton as he can get into his pickup. The town is ready for both, and everyone in between.

Equipment is another marvel. Loom parts abound, and one can buy an empty warp beam for Q. 75 (about $9.75) or one with a jaspe warp already wound onto it for more. The country has just one boat-shuttle maker, and he makes three styles of boat shuttles, all the same size, which cost Q. 35 ($4.50) to 45 ($5.85). Bobbins, made of something that looks like bamboo, are sold by weight, with about one hundred bobbins to the pound, at a cost of Q. 3 ($ .40).

Dyes come in bulk with no instructions except the implied, "ask your father."

What's not in Salcajá is wool. Momostenango is the center of the wool trade, all handspun.

For the first-time visitor, Salcajá can be pretty overwhelming. If the visitor is a weaver, multiply that by ten. It's also really fun.

Chapter 9

DEMETRIO RAMOS
Chiquinom, Momostenango, Totonicapan
K'iche'

At seventy, Demetrio Ramos is not the oldest weaver in the area. But he is the last one weaving the old-style blankets, and he is very proud of that. His growing up was rural; there was no school in the area then. The majority of Demetrio's time was spent working in the fields where his family grew corn, beans, güicoy, and chilacayote. His father was a weaver. At age eight, Demetrio began to wind yarn onto bobbins. At fourteen, he began weaving and has never stopped.

The blankets his father wove were the usual ones of his day, so that's what he taught Demetrio. Demetrio has woven those blankets his whole life. At some point those blankets, called *acordonado*, became the old style. Whereas most style changes are about color or design, the wool blankets of Momostenango have also undergone a structural change that included a possible loom change. Demetrio weaves a four-shaft 2/2 twill in a plaid. The current blankets are two-shaft plain weave with pictures woven in using tapestry or inlay techniques. Because most weavers in Guatemala know how to work in only one style, those who have learned the new style see Demetrio's work as totally mysterious. One man Demetrio knows wants to learn how the old-style blankets are made so that the art will not be lost, but they have not gotten together to do it.

The weave structure and the change from plaid to images play a part in what goes into these blankets. But more than anything else, what is so attractive about the Momostenango blankets is the thick, soft, brushed surface, which begs to be touched and slept under. That luxurious hand comes from two processes, fulling and brushing, or *batanando* and *peinando*.

Momostenango, like much of volcanic Guatemala, sits above rivers of hot water that emerge as hot springs. In Momos, four springs have been corralled into use as baths for both humans and wool blankets. It says a lot about the importance of wool weaving in the area that space for fulling the blankets and rugs is built into the springhouse, one side for humans and the other for blankets and rugs. The spring comes out of the side of the mountain, fills the baths, and from there flows to the river below. (The river is not hot.)

Demetrio fulls four blankets at a time. The walk from his house to where the descent to the spring begins is about thirty minutes. Much harder is the steep climb down to the spring carrying four dry blankets—then the seemingly steeper climb back up carrying four semi-wet blankets. It was easier when he was younger.

In Momos, the fulling process has two basic parts. One involves soaking each blanket in that hot, hot water and scrubbing it with soap. The other involves an amazing one-man dance that lasts at least eight minutes per round. During that "dance,", Demetrio folds, rubs on concrete, rotates the cloth, then folds it to a new arrangement, all using only his bare feet. He does this over and over until all sections have been equally rubbed several times. Three things make fulling happen: extreme temperature shock, abrasion, and a basic solution, such as soap. The soap Demetrio uses is a round brown ball about the size of a baseball called jabon de coche—pig soap. Made from pork lard, it is surprisingly odor-free, and it covers the smell of both powdered detergent (should he use any) and of wet wool.

The process is repeated at least four times: soak and agitate in the hot pool, lift out and scrub with soap, fold up and do the dance, then start over. What the words don't relay is what really hard work it is, and how uncomfortably hot the water is on his

Opposite: Demetrio Ramos and the loom he has been weaving on his whole life.

Opposite: The overhead pulleys support the shafts in the same manner as Emilia's cinta loom (page 48), but Demetrio has four treadles. The single-ply wool warp is sticky enough, and the tension on the warp loose enough, and the weft bobbin fat enough, that the shuttle can only be pushed through the shed a few inches at a time.

Left: Foot looms in Guatemala have few, if any, metal parts. It's all wood, rope, and string—handy for quick fixes. Even the reed on this loom is made of bamboo.

Below: Bobbins of weft ready for boat shuttles specially designed to take such fat bobbins.

feet. Well before he finishes, Demetrio is pouring sweat, and not only from the heat of the water.

Once the fulling and stretching to the right size and shape are complete, Demetrio presses and shakes out all the water he can in preparation for the long climb back up the hill.

Demetrio and his wife, Paula, both grew up in weaving families and both learned to weave. Demetrio says his father's teaching method was by command. He would demonstrate once, then Demetrio and his siblings were expected to know. The family had two looms for two parents and four children, all of whom wove, so they took turns. Because Demetrio and his wife have had only one loom, Demetrio has always been the weaver in the family.

He also learned to spin, though he doesn't do so now, and to dye, which he still does. Most of the wool Demetrio uses is natural-colored: white, gray, and dark brown. He dyes small amounts of light brown, dark blue, and deep red to use as accent colors, using aniline dyes and ashes from the stove. The warp and weft are both single-ply, with the warp finer and spun in the Santa Lucia la Reforma area, and the weft thicker and spun in and around Momos. He goes to the Sunday market in Momos to sell his blankets. He can make four a week and he always sells them all. Then he buys more yarn for the next blankets. He says that the worst problem for blanket and rug sales now is contraband goods coming in from Mexico. Although the Mexican products are not the same quality, they are a lot cheaper so many people buy them.

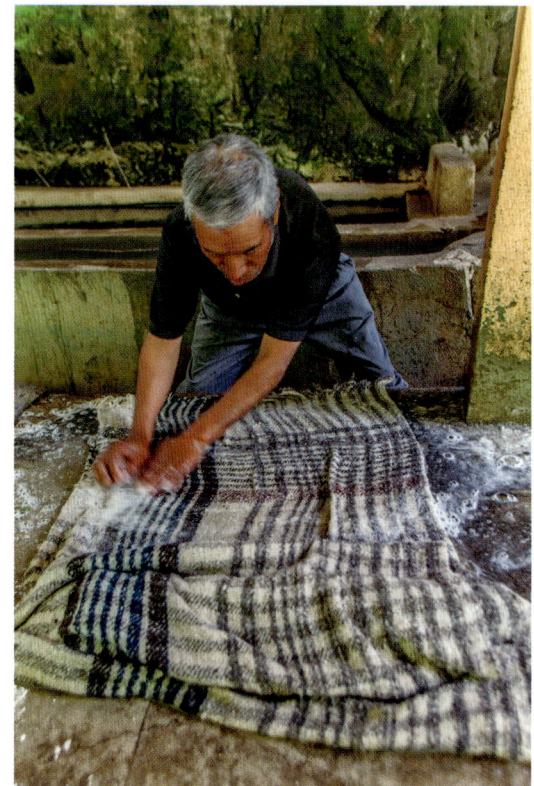

Of the eight children born to Demetrio and Paula, four sons and one daughter are still alive. They have been blessed with twenty-two grandchildren. One son lives a day away on the other side of the country, but the rest all live close by. None of them are weavers, all preferring to have more lucrative careers.

On the day we arrived to take pictures and enjoy another day with Demetrio and Paula, there was a great deal of activity. Many women were coming and going, children were playing, and as always, the focus was on the kitchen. It was March, and we learned that Paula had died at Christmas time. She had not felt good and her skin had turned yellow, so they took her to the health center. After giving her an exam, the doctor told them that she had "tumors or something" and that there was nothing he could do. He said they could take her to the hospital in Totonicapan, an hour and a half away, but it would be por gusto—for nothing—because there was nothing to be done. So they took Paula home and stayed with her until she died at 11:30 a.m. on December 23rd. All the activity when we were there involved preparing food for the next day. It was the day they were going to put the cross on her grave, so there would be a mass at the church first, then the walk to the cemetery, the placing of the cross, and praying. After the service, they would return to

Left: A waterfall in the cold river below the hot springs. Center and Right: After thoroughly soaking the blanket in hot water Demetrio scrubs it hard with jabon de coche. The gap between the pool of hot water and the walkway above is wide enough for him to stand in to work without having to lean over too much. The fulling dance is harder than it looks, and hotter. By the end, Demetrio, seventy, is sweating from the workout. On a good day he can full four blankets, a week's production.

the house to eat *kanac*, the local version of tamalitos.

Demetrio looked good that day, healthy and upbeat. His daughter told me that it was because of all the activity. About a month before, she said, he had passed a barrier of acceptance that now he was a widower. But even though she and a brother live close by and someone spends time with him daily, he lives alone and it's hard. After fifty years of marriage, he misses Paula terribly. He consoles himself by caring for her chickens, and he keeps busy weaving, but still he cries because he misses her.

Demetrio told us that he likes the old designs, and he likes to earn money. Maybe more important now are two other things he told us previously: the weaving is in his heart, and he feels it is a way out and onward forever.

Chapter 10

MARCELINO EMILIO XILOJ DE LEON
Parramus, Momostenango, Totonicapan
K'iche'

First: plant corn. Second: spin the wool and weave rugs to take to market. Third: perform community service. That was the busy life of Marcelino Xiloj. And he still likes to keep busy. But at seventy-eight, with failing eyesight and hearing, he's taking it a little easier. "I don't like to rest. I like to be busy so that time passes more quickly. But I've used up my strength; I don't have much energy." These are the words of a man who now spins even with diminished vision and weaves only one or two hours at a time because he tires more easily.

Plant the corn. Whether the corn is planted and tended by the men or the women, the family *milpa* (cornfield) is one of the most important economic elements of family life. A family of six, such as Marcelino's, will go through about 163 kilograms (360 pounds) of corn in a month. Plant the corn.

Marcelino learned to spin when he was seven and to weave when he was thirteen. These two skills have provided his life's work. Although most of the good wool-producing sheep in Guatemala are in Huehuetenango, turning that wool into rugs and blankets happens mostly in and around Momostenango. Depending on each weaver's circumstances and preferences, he or she will spin more or less of the wool needed. In Marcelino's case, the rugs he wove needed several thicknesses of yarn. Some he spun, some he bought. Likewise, he dyed some of his yarn and bought some already dyed.

The blankets that Marcelino wove were called acordonado; they were the same kind Demetrio (see pages 68-73) still weaves. The difference is that when Marcelino wove them, they had not yet achieved the status of "the old style." Over the years, Marcelino has woven two kinds of rugs. Both are pile rugs using the ghiordes or rya knots, though when he speaks of them, he simply uses the word "knots." *Ralo* or *raja* is the name given to the more loosely woven rugs. They're woven with an inch of flat weaving (plain weave), then a row of knots, another flat inch, and another row of knots. These rugs are very soft and flexible, not good for heavy traffic but oh-so-comfortable beside a bed. The tighter version is called *tupido*. It is made the same way, but with far less space between the rows of knots, making it a sturdier rug.

The knots are tied with *mechas,* pieces of yarn precut to the proper length. Marcelino told us that he learned to cut the mechas with scissors, but his first wife taught him how to do it with a machete, a much faster method. Some rugs are woven of just one color; others have images woven in. When Marcelino knows that he'll be weaving figures of some kind, he cuts his mechas in the colors and quantities he'll need. It's a visual treat to see baskets full of different-colored skeins of yarn on one side of his workshop and on the other side little piles of colored mechas sitting on the weaving-in-process, within easy reach of the weaver.

Marcelino learned to spin on a *torno*, a belt-driven spindle wheel made of wood that has been the local spinning tool since the shift from supported hand spindles more than fifty years ago. Now, the smaller solid wood wheels of the torno are being replaced by shiny new bicycle wheels with a multiple gear system that spins much faster. Marcelino took a workshop in how to use the *ruedina* (the new wheel) eight years ago and proudly displays his certificate on the wall. The spindle wheel also serves as a good fast bobbin winder, so foot loom weavers who don't spin have them as well.

Marcelino spent a lifetime supporting his family through weaving and his community through service.

Cutting mechas. The top end of the machete fits into a crack in the wooden post, the bottom end is braced by his body. Grasp a fistful of yarn well-lined up and slice it on the sharp edge of the machete blade. Definitely faster than scissors, and more accurate, too. The yarn used for the knots is fatter than the weft for the flat areas. The yellow knots are the beginning of the picture he'll weave.

In addition to planting corn and weaving rugs, Marcelino has been active in local politics. He says he likes the contact it gives him with people in his community. Each municipio has an elected mayor. That person is the most important elected official in most people's lives because he operates at the local level. The *alcalde* (mayor) has a geographically large area to tend to, so he appoints assistants to be liaisons with aldeas throughout his district.

Marcelino was first the *alguacil* (sheriff) for Parramus, his aldea. His responsibilities included delivering official papers to people, responding to complaints, and making announcements by walking through the village and speaking in a loud voice.

From aguacil he moved up to *regidor*, the assistant to the *alcalde auxiliar* (assistant mayor). He says that the alcalde auxiliar does not actually do anything himself; he directs other people to do things. The regidor is one of those who carries out his orders. Eventually, Marcelino became the Alcalde Auxiliar himself, the highest non-elected position anyone can have. All of these posts have one-year terms. Marcelino was appointed to the job of alcalde auxiliar four times.

Now Marcelino's community spirit has led him to be on the *Consejo de Ancianos*, the Council of Elders. This body of forty men and women help to resolve conflicts, be they in the community, between neighbors, or between spouses. He says the Council's primary goal is to help people see things from different perspectives, to learn how to think differently. On one of our visits, he had to leave early because the Consejo was meeting with a married couple that was struggling.

Having been married for about sixty years altogether, Marcelino knows something about marriage. As was the custom when he was young, his parents arranged his marriage. When he was eighteen, he married his first wife. They were married for seven years during which she had four children, all of whom died, as did she soon after the last one was born. The next year, his parents arranged another marriage. This was to Florencia Real Culux, who now, more than fifty years later, is still with him. Together, they had nine children, of whom five died. Of the four remaining children, one daughter and one son live close by, one daughter lives in Totonicapan, and the other son lives in the United States.

Teodoro, the son who lives next door, provides whatever physical help his parents need, as well as some financial help. He learned a lot about community service from his father, and the focus of his adult life has been to help weavers and spinners by educating both the public about their textiles and the artisans about better methods for working.

José, the son who lives in the United States, left just four years ago. He is forty-seven, with seven children to support, and weaving was not providing an adequate income. Now, working as a cook, he can financially support his wife and children as well as contribute substantially to his parents' finances.

Marcelino has worked hard and is tired. But perhaps his work with the Consejo reminds him of an additional point of view: "Now, I don't worry about anything. In the past, I had a lot of work, and I earned money. Now, I just see life as peaceful."

THE PEOPLE OF THE CORN

Corn is everything to the Maya. It is not just the staple of life, it is life. The Popol Vuh story of the creation of the world tells that after several unsuccessful attempts with different materials, humans were finally successfully created from corn. The four colors of corn—white, yellow, red, and black—are an integral part of Mayan ceremonies, and all are sacred.

No part of the corn plant ever goes to waste, starting with food: *tamales* (*masa* with meat and sauce inside, soft), tamalitos, tortillas, atol, *boxbol* (masa wrapped in *güisquil* or *ayote* [squash] leaves with a squash seed and chile sauce poured over them), medicinal teas (made with corn silks), and of course *elote* (corn on the cob, roasted, boiled, or cooked in soups). Even a corn plant that produces no corn has value. The leaves are used to wrap tamalitos; the stalks become fences, walls, or animal food; the corncobs are used as firewood and to make toys; and the husks get used for wrapping *chuchitos* (tamalitos with meat and salsa inside, firm) or making dolls. In addition, the growing cornstalk provides both shade and a pole for beans and other food plants.

Photo: Patrycja Zboch/shutterstock.com

Chapter 11

ANA PU FERPUAC

Pamaría, Santa Lucia la Reforma, Totonicapan
K'iche'

A family of wool spinners goes to the coast to pick cotton. They bring home some seeds and plant them. When they have cotton, they spin it, then use the thread for a drive band for their spinning wheel to spin more wool.

To get to the community of Pamaría from Momostenango is about an hour's drive at 15 mph. The slow pace lets one enjoy the spectacular views that create the feeling that one is crossing the top of the world. Along the way are pine trees abundant with sap, with diagonal slashes that let the sap run out. The sap is collected by the makers of *pom* (incense of various kinds). Another tree has had its bark completely removed; those who use the bark insist that its loss does not kill the tree. The reddish bark is chopped up and mixed with the sap, and the resulting *copal* is used as incense in Mayan ceremonial fires. Making pom is one of the two income-generating activities in the municipio of Santa Lucia la

Reforma. The other is spinning wool to be used as warp in the blankets and rugs of Momostenango.

Spinning by the age of eight, married by fifteen, and widowed at thirty, Ana Pu, now seventy-four, supported her children by spinning. As her grandparents had taught her parents and they had taught her, she spun on a torno, a solid wooden wheel that turns a spindle by which the wool fibers are twisted into yarn. She was able to spin 1.7 kilograms (almost 4 pounds) of wool a week. "She was a really fast spinner," her son Juan smiles. The wool market is in Momostenango, a five-hour walk away in those days before roads. Because Ana needed to take care of her children, a trusted neighbor took her yarn to sell and brought raw wool back to her for her next spinning. Those sales provided her only cash income.

Like many others who needed a cash income, Ana, her husband, their children, and extended family used to go to the coast to pick cotton or coffee. They went for one to two months each year, walking eight days to get there. Over the course of those years, Ana had seven children, four of whom died before they were five years old. Then, Ana's husband got a fever that lasted a month before he died from it. That left Ana with three children under eight years of age to raise alone. She chose to never re-marry, knowing that her children would be relegated to a lower status than children from another marriage. She was not willing for that to happen. Being so small, the children were not yet ready to work the land, so it lay fallow for nearly ten years. Ana's own family lived too far away to help; her arranged marriage had moved her to the other side of the municipio. She was too busy to get involved in the church or any other organization, so she was truly on her own.

The land Ana inherited from her husband is fully productive now—trees full of lemons, limes, oranges, and bananas, vines of

Opposite: Brown pom cakes are part of the base ingredients for a Mayan fire ceremony.

Left: Ana spins on a ruedina. It works in the same way as a colonial American great wheel, the principle difference being that instead of a large spoked wooden wheel that is turned by pushing on the spokes, the ruedina uses a converted bicycle wheel with a handle.

Above: Raw wool is carded to separate the locks of wool. Once open and fluffy, it is rolled off the hand cards as rolags, cigar-shaped pieces ready to spin easily.

güisquil (a green squash-like vegetable), turkeys, and corn—this is just some of what is growing now. Ana, her son Juan, and his family live together in a house they built near the one they lived in all those years. And they still spin.

Some things have changed. Twelve years ago, a real road was built to the community. Seven years ago, the community got water and electricity. And three years ago, the family got a ruedina. Things are definitely looking up.

A ruedina functions the same way a torno docs. The big wheel is turned by hand; via a bicycle chain, it turns a spindle; the yarn is spun off the tip of the spindle. The difference with the ruedina is that the drive wheel, a bicycle wheel, is much bigger than the wooden torno wheel, and several gears add to the wheel-to-spindle ratio. The final effect is to double the speed, double the yarn output, and double the income. There are three spinners in the family, Ana, Juan, and Juan's wife Eva, who learned to spin from Juan. (Eva comes from a family of pom makers.) The three of them take turns so the wheel keeps going as much of the time as possible. Together they produce 3.4 kilograms (7½ pounds) of single-ply wool warp per week. If they had another ruedina, they could produce double what they do now. Contraband rugs and blankets coming in from Mexico create a real problem. That competition is driving many weavers out of business, and fewer weavers means less demand for yarn. Nevertheless, Ana believes that the recognized superior quality of her yarn would let her sell twice what she currently spins.

Now that there is a road, pickups offer transportation. To ride in the back of one to and from Momostenango costs Q. 20 ($2.60) round trip. Taking into account that cost plus the cost of raw wool, Ana and family earn Q. 80 ($10.40) per week. A second

ruedina certainly would help, but a ruedina costs Q. 750 ($97).

We asked if they had ever thought of doing something with the yarn themselves. Given that they have some land, we also asked if they had ever raised sheep to supply their own wool. The answer to both questions was no. Spinners spin, weavers weave, and shepherds have sheep. Moreover, warp spinners spin warp, weft spinners spin weft.

When Juan was growing up—without roads, water, or electricity—there were also no schools. The closest one was in Momostenango, that same five-hour hike away. Now, Juan's ten-year-old son, Santiago Enrique, is in third grade, the first one in the family ever to go to school. He loves it. His little sister Ana Cristina, who is just three and a half, had a not uncommon reaction to us: women not wearing traje. She thought we had come from the health center to give her shots. After many assurances to the contrary, she was curious instead of frightened.

We asked Ana, Eva, and Juan what they would like to say to other spinners who might read their story and how they felt about our visit. Ana answered, "I didn't know there were any other spinners. If they want to come and visit, I'd like to share ideas." Eva said, "I'm grateful for your visit. Greetings to any other spinners!" And Juan added, "It's exciting to have you here. We don't get visitors from the outside. I'm also happy you came because the neighbors said it was a lie that you would come and it isn't!"

Ana learned to spin on a hand spindle as a child, but even then her parents had already been using a torno, the wooden wheel that was used before the ruedina. The mechanical advantage of the ruedina's gears, such as those used for bicycles, explains how the ruedina goes so much faster than the torno.

Santiago Enrique also started spinning early. His skill is evident as he spins wool on a much lighter spindle designed for spinning cotton.

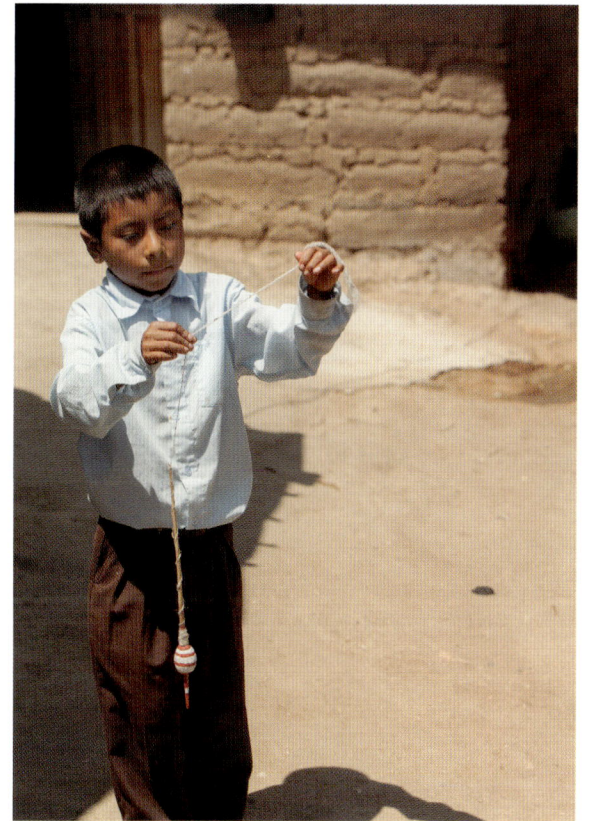

Chapter 12

ANA CETO
Santa María Nebaj, Quiché
Ixil

Ana Ceto, seventy-two, was born in the aldea of Janay, about half an hour from Nebaj, where she lives now. Her mother started to teach her to weave when she was ten. And like so many young Maya girls, she would take the sheep and goats to the fields, and as they grazed, she wove. In that way, she learned to weave the textiles of daily life: huipils, *pantalones* (men's pants), *cotones* or *chaquetas* (men's jackets for ceremonial occasions), fajas, rebozos and *perrajes* (scarves and shawls), servilletas, and the item that so uniquely identifies Nebaj, the cinta. Only cortes were woven by men, on foot looms. Ana moved into the town of Nebaj when she was fourteen, got married at fifteen, and had her first child at sixteen. She eventually had seven children, and she describes her life as "cooking, weaving, cooking, weaving, cooking, weaving...."

"Weaving has always called to me, and I still want to weave. Now, I'm a little tired, but I don't like to just sit and not do anything either. I weave some and do other things."

From the beginning, selling her weaving was Ana's work. She sold huipils for between Q. 100 and Q. 200 (about $13 to $26). At that time, the designs, which are now considered the old style, had straight rows of figures with lines between them, all very orderly. The images were a mix of animal and human figures and geometric designs like diamonds or zigzags, with a lot of the base cloth showing. Most Nebaj huipils have a white foundation, but they can be black or red or whatever color a woman wants. There is no significance to the color, only preference.

As the years passed and the styles changed, the lines between the rows disappeared, and the sizes of the figures got mixed. And though the figures stayed in line for a while, it was as if the gates of the zoo had been opened. Suddenly, there were animals of all different sizes and shapes all over the place, and not a straight line in sight. Although some huipils have a mix of animal and geometric designs, others are exclusively geometric, with lots of diamonds. As new styles come in, old styles continue for some time, so there is a lot of overlap, with many styles present at one time. Ana prefers the old style, and has spent her life weaving huipils for the women who also prefer it.

Above all, Ana prefers to weave sobrehuipiles, the long huipils worn over the daily huipils for three special occasions: weddings, Semana Santa, and the *feria titular*, the town fair celebrating its saint, Santa María. There has been enough demand over the decades for Ana to make that her specialty—ceremonial sobrehuipiles in the old style.

"I wove the wedding clothes for both myself and my husband," she told us proudly, which, given that she married at fifteen, is even more impressive. "Mine was a sobrehuipil like this one I am wearing now. For him, I wove the fabric for his coton, red with black stripes, then took it to a tailor to make the jacket. I also wove the white cloth for his pants, and his belt. Would you like to see how we looked?" Her husband Tomás then left and soon came back wearing the traditional ceremonial traje of men, a red jacket with black pin stripes and designs made in various ways, white pants, and his flashy many-colored woven-diamond belt. After fifty-seven years of marriage, the couple probably looks as beautiful now as they did on their wedding day.

Whether it's designated as a hair wrap, as head gear, or as a headdress, it's called cinta. At 35.6 centimeters (14 inches) wide

Ana at peace
at home.

Ana's sobrehuipil is made of four panels. The front and back are brocaded, the sides plain white. At the bottom you can see her corte, all that shows of the complete traje she is wearing under the sobrehuipil.

The technique of brocade is used to weave designs with a secondary or supplemental weft while the background is woven with a primary or ground weft. Brocade weft can be woven into the surface of the cloth in many ways. On the inside of Ana's sobrehuipil you would see the red and multicolored stripes but only dots of color outlining the birds and other figures..

and 2.7 meters (3 yards) long (or even longer), with big pom-poms on both ends, it would never occur to anyone seeing it on a table that it was to wear in one's hair. The process of wrapping it is so complex that in her wonderful 1976 book of paintings *Maya of Guatemala: Life and Dress* (Guatemala City: Ixchel Museum), Carmen Petterson writes:

Catarina's head-dress looks like a jumble, but is actually very carefully and systematically tied in with her hair. The cloth consists of a long scarf at least 34cm wide with pom-poms loose at both ends. My daughter had to take a series of eight photos of Catarina building it up before I could copy it. Two boys came from this distant village, leaving it for the first time in their lives, to check if I had painted the costume correctly. They burst into joyous laughter at seeing the picture, and then burst into tears. They were homesick and here was a girl from their own pueblo. I was much relieved as I had had great doubts about the head-dress.

Although some women in Nebaj still wear their cinta daily, most do not. Some women don't because it's so heavy that it gives them headaches. On festival days, however, cintas abound, and it is easy to see why they attract so much attention and admiration. They are stunning.

There is no easy transition to the subject of what happened in Ana's family during the Time of Violence. When we asked her

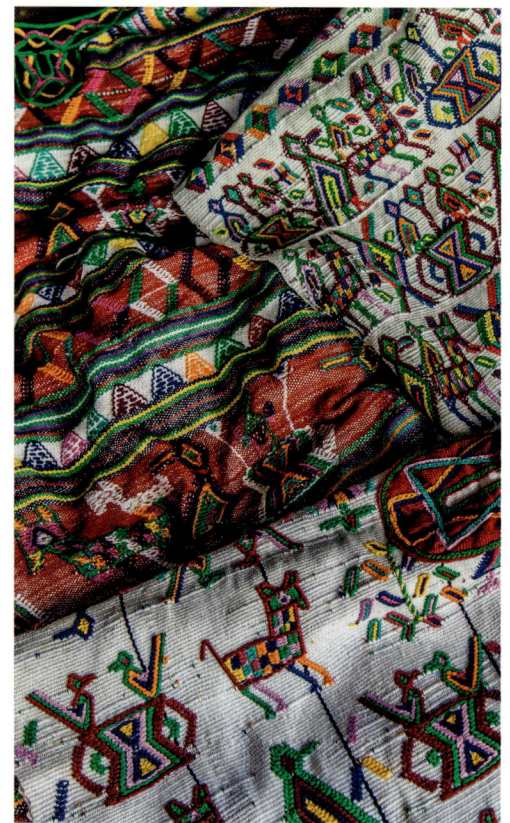

These white huipils are for daily use. The ground fabric is warp-faced, meaning the weft does not show, and it is a much heavier cloth than the sobrehuipil. In the picture with two white huipils, the fashion change is clear. The lower huipil at far right has more white space showing both between rows and within each row. The figures on the body of the huipil are woven brocade. The designs around the neck are all embroidered.

Opposite: Ana's immaculate kitchen and the tinaja she used as a child.

to tell us about it, she became quiet, and in those few moments, her entire body changed. When she spoke, it was as if she were a different person, her brightness gone.

"The part of the family that was still in the village suffered the most. The home where I was born was burned, the animals were lost. One of my brothers was killed and everyone else ran away to Mexico and other places. It was safer in town." She con-

tinued, "Two years later, some came back. My daughter-in-law lost both her parents at age five and was raised in an orphanage with thirty-five other children. It was run by nuns and was a good place. She still has connections there."

After we had all breathed a little, we asked Ana if the figures or colors in the weavings had any special symbolic meaning. First she said no, then said, "Mostly they have no special meaning, except the horizontal zigzag is the mountains. But for me they are reminders of where and when I learned to weave. The mountains were around me, the horse reminds me of the horse we had, the green reminds me of the volcanoes, the blue of the sky, the orange of the rainbow along with purple and all the others. It's nice." A different kind of reminiscence.

And another good memory: When Ana moved from Janay into Nebaj, she had running water in the house for the first time. She no longer needed her *tinaja*, the clay water jug used to carry

water from the source to the house. When Ana got married, she received the tinaja she had used in the village as a gift, not because she needed it but to keep as a reminder of her childhood. Remarkably, Ana still has it, in perfect condition except for one small crack with a patch over it. The tinaja is still beautiful.

Ana and her husband were elected to the *Cofradía* four times. It's a one-year term of office for husband and wife pairs. Being a *Cofrade* is an important role in the community. Originally created by the Catholic Church as a liaison between the church and the Mayan spiritual community, this brotherhood still exists with essentially the same responsibility. Ana's primary job was to organize and oversee the food preparation and related matters for the celebrations. These ceremonies include not only the Cofradía but the whole community, so making sure enough food is in the right places at the right time is a huge job.

The qualities that led Ana and Tomás to be Cofrades are probably the same ones that led them to make sure their children were well educated. Neither Ana nor Tomás ever went to school. Yet all of their children have professional careers. One of their daughters died when she was thirty-four, so Ana and Tomás are raising her children. The oldest of them is starting his university studies in agronomy this year. Ana taught her daughters how to weave; of the two living, one still weaves on a backstrap loom, the other is a nurse and also works with her husband making palm-leaf hats, so she doesn't weave anymore. Ana's granddaughter knows of weaving from Ana, but along with going to school, like her mother, she helps with the family hat business.

We asked Ana if there was anything more she would like to tell us. "I am happy you came because it gives me a chance to remember things and share those memories. Everything is so different now. Things cost so much more. There is more [local] violence so I am afraid to go out." Ana's children mostly live in other towns. "I am happy when they come to visit. We have recovered our land, and we like to go there for the fresh air and take a picnic. We have potatoes planted there now."

SEMANA SANTA—
HOLY WEEK

Semana Santa is the most celebrated time of year in Guatemala. Processions carrying scenes from the last week of the life of Jesus of Nazareth, *alfombras* (carpets) lovingly created on the streets for each procession, stops along the route for the stations of the cross, enactments by live people as well as life-sized statuary depicting the story, incense and music to involve more of the senses—these are just some of the elements of the mostly solemn week. Participants and onlookers are Ladino and Maya, Catholic and non-Catholic, men, women, and children. Responsibilities such as carrying the *andas* (platforms that can weigh more than 2,000 pounds) and designing and constructing the *alfombras* (which take hours to create and minutes to scatter) are reverential tasks performed by families or other close-knit groups and which are passed down from generation to generation. Every ritual is an act of devotion, penitence, or the fulfillment of a promise made in response to a miracle granted. Processions are performed all over Guatemala, in small villages as surely as large cities. Born out of the blending of Spanish Catholicism and Maya tradition, Semana Santa brings hundreds of thousands of visitors to Guatemala every year. Colorful, emotional, and powerful, it is the recognition of the event that defines Christianity. To the faithful there can be nothing more important.

This page: Nebaj on Palm Sunday.

Opposite, clockwise from upper left: Nebaj. Church interior before the procession leaves, Rabinal. Burning incense in Salamá. A Jesus depiction in San Miguel Chicaj. A family expressing devotion along the route of the stations of the cross in Rabinal. Jesus is risen in Guatemala City. Women carrying St. Mary in Cobán. A processional band in Guatemala City. Men carrying a heavy *anda* in Cobán. Center: Children in Guatemala City carry an angel effigy.

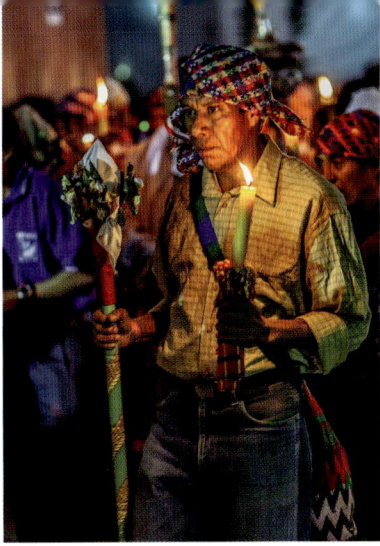

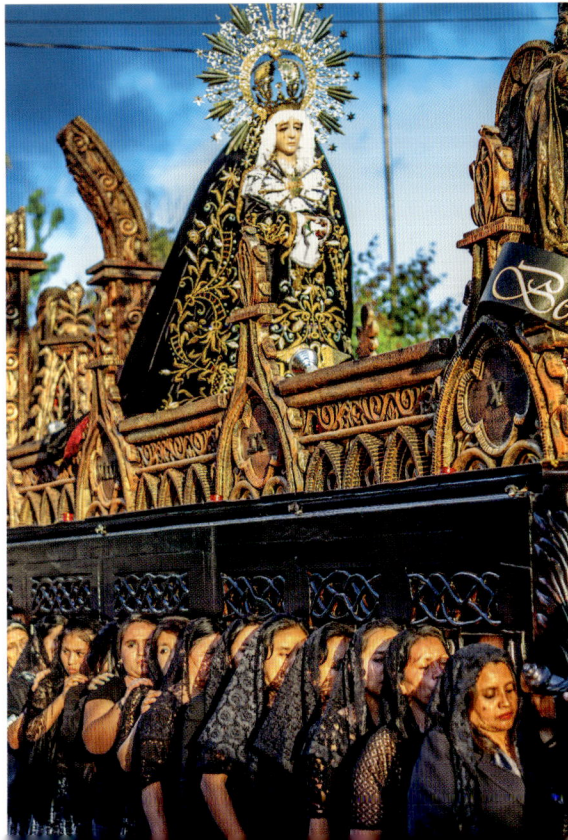

Chapter 13

CATARINA AGUILAR CRUZ

San Juan Cotzal, Quiché
Ixil

On Sabado de Gloria, the day before Easter, it is a tradition called *chiribisco* that parents will take a switch and use it to whip their children to help them grow. In some cases, this switching is general, such as on the backs of their legs so they will grow taller. In other cases, the switching has a more specific intention, as was the case with Catarina's granddaughter, Juana Ireta Garcia Sambrano.

Juana had been begging her mother to teach her to weave, but it never happened. So one day, in secret, she asked Catarina, her *abuela* (grandmother), to teach her. Catarina said yes, and when Juana was twelve and a half years old, they began. It was near Semana Santa. On that Saturday, Abuela Catarina instructed Juana to lay her hands over the cloth on the loom, fingers outstretched. When she did, Catarina took a switch and struck her hands, not too hard, but not too softly either. At the same time, Catarina and Juana each said a prayer asking that Juana become a good weaver. Juana was excited and happy, knowing that now she would learn and become a good weaver.

Catarina, sixty-five, and her husband, Gabriel, had four children. Of those, one died of measles at age eight, one of a stomach problem when in first grade, and the third when it was a month old. The fourth, María, is now thirty-nine; she is Juana's mother, and also a weaver of huipils. María was moved to tears by the thought of Catarina performing the chiribisco with Juana—her mother doing the same with her daughter as she had done with María herself. They all believe that the chiribisco is the secret ingredient that makes their weaving so special, and they may be right; María is a fine weaver and Juana, now thirteen, is an extraordinary weaver. (Catarina says, however, that when she was small, "They whipped me on my head, to make me think better.")

Catarina's home is *muy humilde*, very humble. The room through which you enter is a small tienda selling what the neighbors need. From there you pass into the bedroom, a dark space maybe 2.4 by 4.6 meters (8 by 15 feet), with wood-frame beds on one wall and a low wooden bench on the other. From there, one door leads to the kitchen, with its traditional adobe wood-burning stove and a table and chairs for eating. The second door from the bedroom goes back to a patio that is the same length as the house but narrower in width and has no roof. Beyond the patio is their tiny milpa, which is also home to a few chickens. But humble does not mean without richness; inside that humble home, great things are going on.

Catarina has a passion to teach. It's half of what she talks about. She also loves to weave, especially the older, more traditional patterns. And she loves that she has most of those old patterns in her head already. For what's not in her memory, she can take a very old fabric sample and re-create it just by looking at it. What she wants more than anything is to have help to write a book that would detail all the information in her head so that after she is gone, the information will still be available for weavers-yet-to-come.

Catarina also loves to sell. In her younger days, she left her husband at home and traveled long distances, alone, to sell her weaving. "My husband trusted me. But it's also important for a woman to know her own worth, to create respect for her in others." In those days, traveling in and out of Cotzal was not easy, and she would be gone for days at a time as she went to Chichicastenango, Panajachel, Antigua, and even Guatemala City. Her husband still encourages her to weave something for herself, and at times she starts to. Like now. "This is a replica of an old huipil that I am making for myself. But if someone comes along and

Catarina Aguilar is doing a different kind of brocade. While there are some small figures of distinct colors, most of the design is created by passing the red weft all the way across, alternating with a white weft to create the ground cloth. The flat stick in her right hand is used to hold open the selected spaces for the red weft.

Picking warp threads to be held up or down according to the next pattern weft. The shed stick to hold the space open is at the top of the picture. The larger figure will be a bird, the smaller one a corn plant.

likes it and wants to buy it, I'll sell it." She only weaves the old style, her preference and her market. "The new styles take too long, and besides a lot of weavers are doing those. I weave the older designs, mostly by special order. I can make cintas, huipils, fajas, tzutes, and servilletas—whatever someone wants."

"When I was a girl, I could only weave by special order because I couldn't afford the yarn to weave without having a buyer first. Now, for a special-order huipil that costs Q. 2,500 ($325), I charge a deposit of Q. 500 ($65). When I teach, I use *mish* (20/2 mercerized cotton in skeins), which is less expensive. When I weave to sell or for myself, I use sedalina (DMC perle cotton in little balls)." For a time, Catarina was weaving for a woman named Susana from the United States. Unfortunately, when she spent fifteen days in the hospital with gastritis, her husband did some housecleaning and inadvertently burned the papers that had the contact information for Susana. Catarina has some weaving partly done for Susana but can't reach her to finalize it.

Catarina met Susana through an experience that was the highlight of her teaching life. In a workshop organized by a man named Maximiliano and held in the Cultural Center in Cotzal, Catarina taught twelve women for eighteen months. The class was free for those women, with Maximiliano's only mandate: Learn and produce to sell. "The students only learned to make huipils. They never learned to make servilletas or fajas or the other textiles people need. They needed more classes. There were going to be more, but the organization that was paying for the class stopped. Some of the students dropped out before the end. Only four are still weaving. I hoped that they would share the information with others, but they don't. They are jealous and keep it to

Left: Another style of brocade common in Cotzal. Densely covered, only in the lower left corner is some of the black ground cloth visible. The stripes are made with two colors of yarn twisted together.

One of Catarina's most prized possessions, this is all that was left in damaged church storage of garments made for a saint. The textiles woven for saints in churches were of the highest quality, and provide a valuable historic record. Even with all the damage, Catarina can "read the cloth" and reproduce it.

Belts such as these are woven with or without brocade and may or may not have embroidery added later. Other styles of belts are made as well, many regions having their own. Most curious is their use with corte—or not. In some towns women use belts to secure their cortes. In other places the cortes have drawstrings sewn in, and in others they use no belt at all, they simply pull tight and tuck the pulled corner of the cloth into their waist, as one would with a towel after a shower. Seems risky, but it works.

themselves." Even so, Catarina would love to be teaching again, and knows women who want to learn from her. The problem is that she can't afford to do it without being paid, and the women who want to learn have no money to pay for a class.

In both old and new styles, the figures are the same: birds, plants, birds between birds, and geometric shapes based on diagonals—Xs, horizontal zigzags, triangles, and chevrons. The figures are all in rows, with multicolored straight lines between the rows.

The biggest difference between the older and newer styles is how fully patterned they are. The older huipils are pretty full, but with some space between the figures where the base cloth shows through. In the newer style, the brocaded designs are so packed in that the background cloth is not visible at all. Both are beautiful; each just has a different effect. And Catarina is right, it would take a lot longer to weave the newer style.

Another difference that she mentions is the color palette. The older style has stronger, brighter colors; the newer style has more pastel shades. She prefers the brighter colors, but says that the brighter yarns are harder to get in Cotzal now because the stores carry what sells, and what's "modern" is what sells: pastels. As for the base cloth, in the past nearly all base cloths were white. Now other colors, pastels, are also common.

Also of interest is the different treatment of the center panel and the sleeves. First, they are not necessarily the same colors. Although the body may be a mix of reds, the sleeves can be blue, green, and purple. Second, the sleeves and the body may both be warp-faced or the sleeves could be warp-faced and the body weft-faced.

When Catarina was thirteen, she learned to weave from some elderly neighbors. She noticed early on how huipils that sold in the community for less than Q. 15 ($2) sold to people from the outside for Q. 200 ($26). "That taught me that our huipils had greater value than anyone thought." Catarina is a woman who understands value and where it comes from. The chiribisco performed on her head worked well.

The technique of brocade used in this huipil leaves no yarn on the back (inside) with the exception of some thread ends. Even for the mountains, each line had its own mini-skein of weft. From the back as much as from the front it is very easy to believe that this huipil and the embroidered huipil of Santa Apolonia were created in the same way. It is for this technique specifically that the huipil of Santa Apolonia is sometimes called false brocade. (See page 22.)

Chapter 14

MARÍA RAYMUNDO
San Gaspar Chajul, Quiché
Ixil

Today's huipils from Chajul would be unrecognizable to anyone who had not seen the changes along the way. Forty years ago, the huipils were all white with no added designs. This is the huipil María Raymundo's mother wove. Then a few small figures began to be woven here and there. The figures began to be lined up across the front, not all the same size, but starting on the same row. Gradually, the figures began to grow in size, from about two fingers tall to 15.2 to 20.3 centimeters (6 to 8 inches) tall and nearly as wide. Despite the changes, María's mother continued to weave all white.

María, at age twelve, wanted to learn to weave the new ones, to weave those animals and other figures. Because her mother did not know how, nor did she have colored yarns or money to buy them, she couldn't show María how to do it. So the curious María went to a neighbor and asked if she would buy yarn and order a huipil with designs on it from María, a small one that would be for her daughter. The neighbor said yes, and a new door opened in María's world. When María's mother found out, she was not happy. "What if you can't do it? What if she doesn't like it?" If María got herself into trouble, she said, she would have to get herself out of it.

But María didn't get into trouble. By copying other huipils, she taught herself to weave designs, and the neighbor *did* like the huipil, as did another neighbor, and another, and another. In the years that followed, María became an accomplished weaver of huipils and fajas with and without designs. By the time she was married at seventeen, she had been selling her weaving for years and had become accustomed to earning her own money. Her new husband said she did not need to weave anymore; he could support them and she could avoid the pain that plagues so many weavers. But María enjoyed and continued weaving—for a time for family only. As their children were born, some extra income became necessary, so María was happy to start weaving to sell once again. Again, she asked her neighbors if they needed anything woven. They did, and she has been selling from her home ever since. The quality of her weaving brings people to her door, just as it did when she was twelve years old.

As the designs got bigger, the number of them on a huipil had to be reduced. Now, the majority of huipils have a single large figure on the right and left sides of the front and back, plus one more under the arm on each side (six total). With one large bird or horse on each side of the huipil (left and right), the two may face each other or face in the same direction. There is additional patterning on the shoulders and arms, mostly geometric designs.

Even more surprising is what has happened to the colors. From the white base with no other color that Marías's mother wove, huipils went to having a background of red, then blue. Now, the background is whatever color the wearer wants, including white. More colors keep coming into fashion, but the old ones don't go out, so walking through Chajul now is like walking through a yarn store, with huipils of red, lime green, sky blue, maroon, turquoise, yellow, and more. And those are just the solid background colors. The figures themselves have even more colors, and the principle seems to be the more the better. Although the size of a horse or bird on the right side is the same as its mate on the left, the colors may be not only different, but a riot of colors throughout.

According to María, "There are also changes in which designs are popular, whether it's ducks, geese, horses, eagles, or other birds. When I got married, my mother gave me a huipil with dia-

María Raymundo with three of her eight children. In these modern times it is common for some girls to wear traje and some not, or for some occasions but not others, even in the same family. Note that María's hair wrapping is different from that in other communities.

This is the style of huipil that
the twelve-year-old María
taught herself to weave.
Before this they were all
white, with no figures. Over
the years they have evolved
and now the figures fill the
entire huipil, which comes
in every color available.

María's daughter. She does not always wear one, but she is learning how to weave huipils from her mother.

monds on it. To me that was already out of fashion, and because I was a teenager, I didn't like it." She continued, "the *k'ot* (double-headed eagle) is always the most important figure to us, but it has also evolved. First, its wings were made with diamonds and were folded down, close to its body. Then, they opened up half way. Now, they're completely open."

Not only does María love to weave, she also loves to share her knowledge. When they were children, María taught her sister to weave designs, and together they brought a useful income into the household. Now, as a mother, she is teaching her daughters to weave. As they have gotten old enough to enjoy weaving their own huipils with the designs and colors they like, María has gained time to weave pieces to sell. She weaves what women ask her to, in the colors and styles they want. For a plain white huipil, she supplies the yarn and it takes her about fifteen days to weave it. For a colored huipil with figures on it, the buyer supplies the yarn. That huipil takes her about a month to weave.

These are not eight-hour days. María has eight children, four daughters and four sons. The bigger ones help take care of the smaller ones and help with other household chores, but there is still plenty to do. (The accepted belief in rural Guatemala is that a woman who has only two children has a lot more work to do than a woman who has ten; only two means they're small and the mother has to do everything, but with ten, some are big and can help with the work.) María's children attend school, and for that María has come to be connected to Limitless Horizons Ixil (LHI), an organization that provides scholarships in the Chajul area. Recognizing that the families they work with need greater income, LHI has started a marketing program to sell the work of the mothers of their scholarship students. In that program, they have three *Mamás de Emergencia,* Emergency Mothers who can

weave samples quickly, reliably, and of high quality. María is one of the Mamás.

"Weaving for Limitless Horizons is steady work, with orders every month. I usually have orders for about ten scarves or other products per month, except in September, when I weave things for my kids for the fair and parades for Independence Day. The 'emergency' weaving comes when it comes, and that is good too." Through her work with LHI, María has learned what products and designs appeal to the export market. Weaving the samples also helps provide the income that allows her to keep weaving quality traditional work for her family.

We asked María about the tradition of certain colors or designs indicating who is single or married. "We don't have any of that, but the younger girls want brighter colors, shorter sleeves, and more open necks." We asked if that meant that they basically wanted more skin showing. "Yes," she agreed. "The older women are more likely to want softer colors, those that were in fashion when they were young. And when someone dies, the burial huipil will be white, but it can have any design in any color."

María also weaves the old designs and colors for her mother-in-law, who is seventy-five and can no longer see well enough to weave. Because María actually prefers weaving smaller designs, she's happy that the latest fashion has the designs shrinking again. When she was a young girl learning to weave, she wove a huipil for herself, but because the family always needed more income, her mother made her sell it. Recently, remembering it, she rewove it. Finally, she has one like the first one she wove for herself. Thinking back, María tells us, "When I was twelve years old, I just wanted to learn something new, to experiment." Little did she imagine that the "something new" would become so much a part of her life.

While the technique and idea of Chajul huipils is consistent, there is individuality at play. The birds' wings have different designs, the neck openings of María's green huipil and the red one she is holding are different shapes, as are the borders of the shoulder patches. And finally, or first, is color, which celebrates the whole color spectrum.

THE K'OT—
THE TWO-HEADED EAGLE

The history of the k'ot in the Americas is as varied and intriguing as the myths themselves. Used as a symbol in weaving long before the Spaniards arrived, the two-headed eagle represented the dualities of life—looking forward and back, seeing good and evil, looking up to the heavens and connecting to the earth. To the Maya, the balance is complementary, all part of their worldview.

The Spaniards arrived with their own two-headed eagle, this one a European symbol of the Spanish Habsburgs and of the Guild of Weavers of Wool, Linen, and Cotton. As part of their ongoing effort to stamp out paganism, the conquerors forbade any expression of the k'ot. At the same time, as a special reward recognizing the bravery of the K'iche' warriors, they allowed them to adopt the Hapsburg symbol.

So the K'iche's continued to weave this symbol of duality, to the Spanish a sign of submission and to the K'iche's a sign of subversion.

In keeping with the dual nature of the k'ot, the myths show this figure as both a threat to and a rescuer of the Maya people. There are many versions of the tales; here are two:

The k'ot was eating people at random; no one was safe. The people took to wearing boards tied to their backs so that if they were caught and lifted up they could untie themselves and escape. A man decided he would kill the k'ot, so he took his machete and allowed himself to be eaten. Once the k'ot had flown back to his own nest the man killed him from the inside. Then the man freed himself and killed all the other k'ots nearby.

The k'ot was the defender of the people, fighting to protect them from outside threats. One time, there was a war. He was fighting in a fierce battle, but the enemy had guns. The k'ot fought hard for a long time. Finally, they shot him and he was killed. But he is the k'ot, and he will come back the next time he is needed to help defend his people again.

Chapter 15

VICENTE LAINEZ CABA

San Gaspar Chajul, Quiché

Ixil

Baskets/*canastas*
Wicker/*mimbre*
Vine/*bejuco*
Being your own boss/*excelente*

Vicente Lainez, forty-five, is a gentle man for whom family is clearly central to life. His father made baskets until he was eighty-five or ninety, and lived well past one hundred. Vicente learned to make baskets from his father when he was eight years old, as did his four brothers. He is now teaching his older son, Pedro, a teenager, but he tells us, "It is taking longer because he goes to school." His little boy, Manuel, does not yet have the manual dexterity required, but he sits at his dad's feet and plays at making baskets with the materials at hand. When his hands are ready, the knowledge will already be within.

Stepping from the bright sunlight into the dark unlit room indoors takes some visual adjustment. Even so, it is easy to see that Vicente's baskets, both large and small, are handsome and well made. They reflect generations of fine craftsmanship. As our eyes adjusted, we could appreciate the details as well.

All of the materials for the baskets grow nearby and are available during both the rainy season and the dry season—an important factor because each season lasts six months. Mimbre grows more in the lower, warmer area around neighboring San Juan Cotzal than in the higher altitude of Chajul, so Vicente buys it from a friend who collects and sells it for Q. 25 ($3.25)/pound regardless of its thickness. With thick mimbre, Vicente makes bigger baskets; with thin mimbre, he makes smaller baskets, even miniatures. All sell well.

The mimbre is what goes around the basket. The spines or spokes of the basket, which the mimbre is woven into, are made of a bejuco (vine) that is thick enough so that one vine can be sliced lengthwise into spokes for two or three baskets, and moist enough so that it can be sliced with a kitchen knife. Every basket, regardless of size, has seven strips of bejuco going from one side to the other, so fourteen spokes to weave the mimbre through.

Vicente collects his own bejuco, walking an hour and a half to a place where there is an endless supply. In one trip, using a *mecapal* (tumpline, headstrap), he can carry out enough to make either forty-eight big baskets or eighty-four small ones. Depending on what other tasks he has, he makes the three-hour round-trip trek once every seven to fifteen days.

The final decorative wrapping around the top edge of the basket uses the *corteza de pin* (the bark of the vine), which comes in varying shades of red-orange. If it is not dark enough, it's dyed with *achiote*, a plant with red seeds that also color and flavor food. "The wrapping isn't necessary, but the people like the colored rim and the baskets sell better with it," he told us. Vicente's wife does not make baskets, but she does give them their final touch, wrapping the edge.

"My father did not own any land, so we had to earn money to be able to buy corn. I now have a milpa (cornfield), but it is not enough to feed my family, so I continue making baskets. I figured out early on that I could not earn enough selling only my own baskets, so now I also sell the baskets of others. Some live here, some live farther away. Our primary market is *ferias titulares* (town fairs). My wife and I travel to all the bigger towns, including Totonicapan, Quetzaltenango, Tecpan, Antigua, and Quiché. Other than that we sell in front of the church, which is good for us because it is only two blocks away. The church draws a lot of pilgrims."

The front door of the church in the park where they sell their baskets is of light-colored wood with a grid carved top to bottom. Each square in the grid has a carved symbol. Most are familiar-looking Mayan glyphs, but the most important symbol to the history of the Ixil is the k'ot, a two-headed eagle. The k'ot carved

Growing in the wild, each roll of vine or wicker has unique characteristics. Reading and understanding those characteristics is important in deciding which size and style of basket to make.

A multigenerational skill, the steps in making baskets that Vicente and his brothers learned from their father are the same ones he is passing on to his sons.

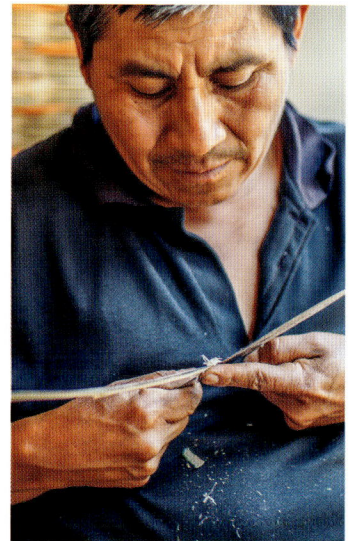

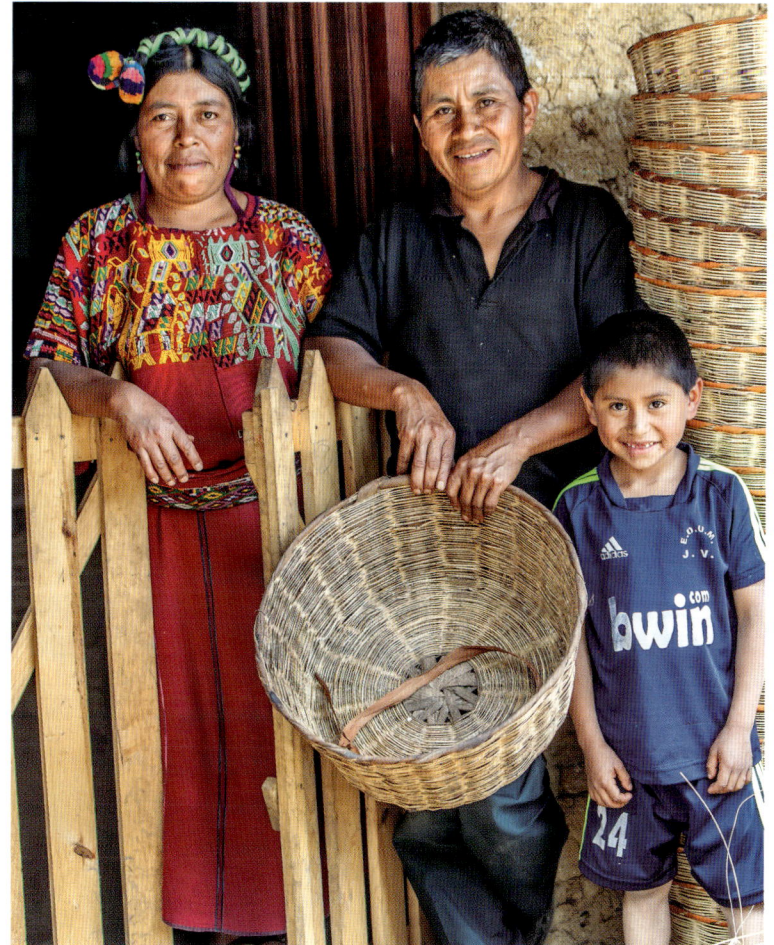

on the door of the church—with a cross as part of the design—reflects the joining of two traditions. (See more on the k'ot on page 101.) Perhaps the beauty of the door helps the pilgrims see the beauty of the baskets.

"My wife sells the baskets there or brings visitors to the house to buy. Lately, we have thought it might be good to have a sign on the house that says we sell baskets. It's a new idea. I could never have done it before because I never went to school and so I don't know how to read and write. Now that my son is going to school, he could make the sign."

When we asked Vicente if he makes baskets only because it's a living or if he loves making baskets, he said, "I do like making baskets, and it is also my livelihood. I definitely prefer making baskets to any other kind of work. I like being my own boss." Because his sons are going to school, they will have options that Vicente and his brothers never had. But they will also have the option of carrying on the family tradition of making baskets that give the gifts of both beauty and function—whether for work or pleasure.

Chapter 16

DOMINGO ASICONA

San Gaspar Chajul, Quiché
Ixil

Don Domingo is an *encantador*, an enchanter. At eighty-nine, he has a sly grin that suggests a lifetime of mischief-making. He has many kinds of stories—like when he was a boy and it was his job to take the cows out to pasture, on leads. "The cows were big and I was small. Three times they ran away with me and three times I cried." Serious business for an eight-year-old.

When Domingo was growing up, every family, every household, made whatever it needed. That included hats made of palm leaves that were braided and then sewn by hand, *morrales* (shoulder bags) made from *maguey* that grew on their land, handwoven huipils, and whatever other cloth they needed in the home. And, of course, food for a household of nine. His education came from the land. "My school was in the fields—cleaning, cutting trees, planting. I've seen a lot of changes. In those days we used hatchets; now they have chain saws. We had no shoes, even when there was frost on the ground; now they have shoes." As for his grandchildren, the youth of today, "Now the kids go to school and they suffer at their school in their way just like we did in our way. But in the end they have opportunities for work and an income." What concerns him is those young people who get a lot of support and don't have to work so hard for what they have, so they don't know how to use or care for their resources.

Only in the last fifteen years have the roads to and within the Ixil Triangle been paved, making the area far less remote than it used to be. When Domingo was growing up, the only access to Chajul was by horse or on foot; now, one can drive there from Guatemala City in six or seven hours, taking time for lunch along the way.

Geographically, the *Triangulo Ixil* (Ixil Triangle, made up of three towns—Nebaj, Cotzal, and Chajul) is one of the most beautiful areas in an unendingly beautiful country. Altitudes ranging from 1,230 to 2,600 meters (4,000 to 8,500 feet) make for a range of agricultural options, from low-altitude fruit to high-altitude coffee. Especially in San Juan Cotzal, but also in Chajul, maguey production was a major endeavor. Both the fiber (also known as sisal) and the products made from it were sold within and outside of the Triangle. Domingo's father grew maguey, and in addition to the crop, they had all of the equipment needed for extracting the fibers and preparing them for use. For many reasons, mostly economic, maguey production has dropped off all over Guatemala. Domingo's farm was no exception, and without a market, they quit harvesting it. The plants are still there, but nothing is being done with them. Once they no longer processed their own maguey, they bought small quantities of already-processed fiber from Cotzal. Domingo was able to make those purchases until two years ago, when no one brought maguey to town anymore—further evidence of the decline.

Because he could no longer buy maguey, and had had to give up working the land (at age eighty-seven), Domingo decided to continue his work with a new "fiber"—the strips of plastic he can pull out of a *costal*, a big woven synthetic bag used to hold grain, sand, vegetables, and more. Using the same techniques he had used with maguey, he still creates morrales. He also makes larger bags that men carry on their backs, held there by mecapals.

Domingo was happy to show us how he works. Starting with a new costal, he trims off both ends, then gently steps into the bag as if he were putting on a skirt. Fishing around to get a good hold on a vertical strip, with some effort, he is finally able to pull up hard and remove the strip from his "plastic" skirt. That strip is carefully laid aside, and then he pulls a second one, which takes

Domingo Asicona—still enjoying life.

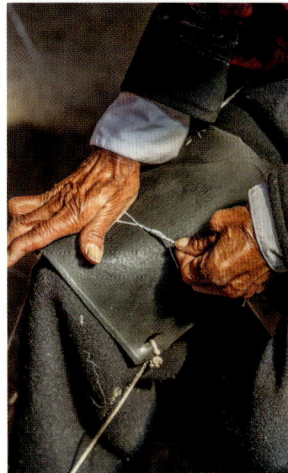

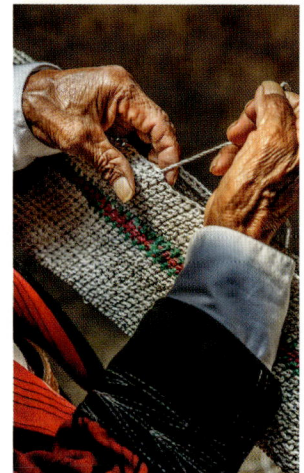

His family grew and worked maguey for their own use. With the maguey gone Domingo uses the same techniques but with a new material—the strips pulled out of synthetic grain sacks.

slightly less effort. The third takes less still, and by the time he gets to number four, it has become easy. He continues to "un-weave" his skirt until all of the vertical strips have been removed and what's left is a stack of loose plastic rings around him. Those get cut in one place to change them from loops to straight strips, and he has the first set of strips for making his morral. It takes six costals to make one morral. He uses only white costals. If he wants colored stripes he buys already-made *pita* in the market. (Pita is synthetic rope that comes in varying thicknesses and lots of colors.)

With his strips ready, Domingo pulls out a really ingenious aid. "We know that the fiber we spin on our legs can hurt our skin, so we figured out that using a patch of an old rubber tire would protect us." He has a patch of rubber approximately 10 by 20 centimeters (4 by 8 inches), with strings tied on both ends in large loops. One loop goes around his waist, the other hooks around his foot, so between the two strings he can hold the rubber patch taut and in place. He then proceeds to spin the strips of plastic on his thigh in the same way that people have been twisting maguey fibers together for centuries. With two separate parallel groups of strips, he first rolls them both from left to right. Once they are sufficiently twisted he then rolls them back from right to left, but together so they wrap around each other, making a two-ply cord.

Although the material is totally different, the finished cord comes out the same size as his maguey strands did. (It's about the thickness of a medium chalking cord.) He twists lengths of roughly 7.3 meters (8 yards) at a time; the strands need to be pulled through loops during the process of making a morral. Longer pieces would be unwieldy; shorter strips would require more splicing.

In Guatemala, four looping techniques are used with maguey; we saw bags Domingo had made using three of them. It takes him about a month to make one morral, which he then sells for Q. 200 (about $26). The women who first introduced us to him said that every day he sits in front of his house—the one he was born in—working on his bags and talking with whoever goes by. At eighty-nine, he is taking life a little easier.

"My father taught me how to work with the maguey, cutting the plants, cooking the leaves in big pots, then using the special tools for scraping and removing the fibers. I watched until I was sixteen, then started to make the morrales. We also made thinner thread for sewing the palm hats." Now his hands are gnarled with arthritis, but he says it is his shoulder that hurts if he works too long.

He was excited about our visit, knowing that we would be taking photographs. He put on his best, most traditional jacket, a coton, red with black pin stripes and additional stitched decorations. This jacket is primarily for ceremonial purposes, and we saw many men wearing them that night in nearby Nebaj because it was Semana Santa. He also wore his palm leaf hat. When we asked if he ever took it off, he said that he always wears it, even did as a boy. "If I took it off, I would be somebody else."

But even more than the picture-taking, Domingo was excited to see us again. He said he didn't know how we found him, but because he had been told we would be back to see him again, he had prayed that we would really come. That morning he woke up so excited that he prayed even more that we would actually arrive. As we were getting ready to leave, he asked for all of our names on paper. "With your names, I will pray for all of you for the rest of my life. And when I die, my daughter-in-law will continue praying for you."

A semi-traditional morral, where techniques from centuries past continue into the new millennium.

Chapter 17

AMALIA GÜE
Samac, Cobán, Alta Verapaz,
Q'eqchi'

Amalia Güe, thirty-three, is not the only artisan in this book to have been to the United States, but she is the only one with a son who could come and go as he pleases—if he were not just a year old. Ironically, one of Amalia's dreams is for her eldest daughter to go to the United States so she can teach the *pijbil* style of weaving to interested people there. But all of that is part of the maybe-future. Let's start at the beginning.

Amalia was born in Simajij, an aldea that at that time had no road and could only be reached on foot. The first of what were eventually eight siblings, she was only four years old when they left Simajij because it had gotten too dangerous. The killings there seemed to be random, and just walking down the road was risky. Her grandfather, killed near the corner of his house, was the only person their family lost during the Time of Violence. They moved to Samac, an hour's walk down the road, but safer. Eventually, they recovered the land they had had to abandon, but they never moved back.

Amalia's grandmother was a backstrap weaver who taught Amalia's mother how to weave, who then taught Amalia, who is now teaching her daughters.

Amalia is the President of the *Grupo de Mujeres Ix Balam Q'ue', Diosa de la Luna* (Group of Women, Goddess of the Moon).

Above: Pijbils—carved bone or wood tools for lifting chosen threads to form designs. The figures on top are a chicken and a *quetzal,* the national bird of Guatemala native to Alta Verapaz.

With sixty members, the group is focused on keeping the traditional weaving technique of their area alive. Pijbil is woven in a number of communities, each with its own variation, but the Samac version is pijbil in its purest—and most challenging—form.

Woven entirely with a 20/1 single-ply non-mercerized cotton, the cloth is a gauzy plain-weave foundation with inlaid designs of plants, animals, small figures of women and men, and geometric forms. What makes the work especially challenging, even aside from working with a single-ply warp, is that all of it is white, background and inlaid figures alike. Challenging and elegant.

The inlaid figures come from the weavers' daily lives. The arch may be a hill, a mountain, a river, or a road. Small dots represent grains of corn, beans, or hail. There are little ducks that look just like Amalia's ducks. Animal paw prints look like those of a dog, but the traditional interpretation is that they're jaguar prints, the jaguar being a sacred animal in Maya cosmology. Designs also include the leaves of the pacaya plant, which is used for special fiestas and ceremonies, especially around the time of Semana Santa, when the plant is mature. Tobacco and corn both attract the hummingbird, and, of course, the spider is the weaver. A star, regardless of how many points it has, is simply a star, often used as a decoration on top of the monstrance in a religious procession.

The inlay is done with a needle-like bone or fine wood pick-up stick that is called pijbil, thus the name of the cloth. Selected warp threads are picked up, and three strands of weft are laid in to create the design. Those three threads together give the designs more substance; even so, the best way to see the picture is to hold the cloth up to the light.

This large room in Amalia's house serves many purposes: bedroom, living room, weaving studio, yarn storage, meeting space, and sometimes dining room for guests. The primary requirement for a place to weave on a backstrap loom is a strong post to tie the loom to. It also has to be high enough, and have enough open distance, to be able to get the correct angle on the warp.

The countryside around Samac. If vertical land is what you have, then vertical farming is what you do.

The community of Samac and the group of women are so far from any markets that it has only been with dedicated help that the world beyond Samac has seen their work. Olga Reiche, a Guatemalan woman who grew up in the area, has been a tireless promoter of the pijbil weavers and their cloth. Having their work in a few good stores in Antigua and now having some international clients as well has been good, but the biggest event by far is their inclusion in the Santa Fe International Folk Art Market. Weaving for that show alone keeps the women working for much of the year, and it gives their traditions and culture great exposure. Amalia has been their representative each year—which is why her son will be able to come and go freely between Guatemala and the United States. When she went to the Folk Art Market in 2013, she was pregnant with an expected delivery date in August. She had miscalculated, and to everyone's surprise—especially hers—she went into labor her second day there. Juan Francisco ended up being born in Santa Fe and so is an American citizen in addition to being a Guatemalan citizen.

Just as baby Juan Francisco will grow up in a world different from his mother's, so the grandmothers in the group grew up in a world different from that of the younger members. Formal education is part of it. Many of the older women never went to school. Amalia only went to first grade and really wishes she had been able to continue. Her six children, three girls and three boys, are all (or will be) in school, leaving Samac to get the best education they can.

Years ago the only use of pijbil weaving was for huipils. Now, to reach that broader market, the women are weaving table runners, scarves, and other items of many different sizes. Part of the art of pijbil is that the designs are centered, both edges being balanced. The older women, who have spent their lives weaving huipils, have those counts in their heads. Want horses? Count this many threads. Want rows of women and men? Count like this. They know many figures and the counts for all of them. The designs are not written anywhere; they are stored in memory. But all the counts are for the width and length of a huipil. If you want something narrower or wider the counts won't work. The younger

Elegant in every way, non-mercerized single-ply white on white is Samac's version of pijbil. The background is woven with one strand of weft, the designs with three strands so they stand out more. Because a single strand of 20/1 thread is so fragile, the warp is sized before being woven by running it through a bath of water with corn or other vegetable starch. The stiffener protects the work in progress and washes out when no longer needed.

women in the group are just the opposite. They can measure and re-calculate where the designs need to be for different-sized finished products, but they don't yet know how to do many figures.

The special hair adornment in Cobán is called a tupuy, and it's distinct from any other. The biggest difference is that it's not woven. Made mostly with red acrylic yarn, the *tupuy* is braided first independently and then into a woman's hair. Also called the coral snake, the tupuy's various legends indicate its significance. Many say that it's a symbol of the connection between humans and the gods. On the other hand, at Amalia's house, where many women were present, they told us that it represents a snake and that the red is for pregnancy.

Years ago, women wore the tupuy all the time, but its use has diminished. At Amalia's house, we saw several. The simplest and smallest were for her daughters to wear to school events. The most elaborate were for Amalia or her older daughters to wear to special events, such as weddings and Semana Santa.

As for traje in general, there is an even clearer distinction between everyday wear and special occasion clothing. For everyday wear, the corte is blue, the huipil—always of pijbil—is white but not fine. A special event will be recognized with black corte, a fine white huipil, and a tupuy. This clothing says that the day is special, the event is special, and the person wearing this traje is special. All have value.

And that's the main message of working to save the purest form of pijbil weaving from extinction. It is beautiful and it represents the culture in many ways; for both of those reasons and more, it has value.

Top left: Juan Francisco (Frankie), American citizen, with his mother and sister.

Bottom left: The tupuy, a hair decoration made of red acrylic yarn, has gone out of use in some places but is alive and well in Samac. Amalia and her daughters have several for different occasions, from simple ones for school events to elaborate and beautiful ones for Semana Santa. Pictured here is one Amalia's daughters wear to special programs at school.

Some History of Samac, Cobán, Alta Verapaz

For the source of the name Samac, there are two theories.

Sa—place, mac—split, the split place

Samat—a local herb used in making *kak iq*, a traditional dish

Between 1871 and 1883, the territory of the Verapaces was declared "unused." President Justo Rufino Barrios appropriated the land from the resident Q'eqchi's and gave it to new tenants. During those years, many Germans arrived and built large coffee plantations. In 1879, there were 170 such fincas, of which one hundred were in Alta Verapaz.

An 1880 census indicated that there were 397 inhabitants dedicated to the cultivation of coffee and sugar cane.

In 1884, Samac was founded. Along with many similar communities, it was part of a huge land-holding of Gustavo Helmerich. He was called the Giant of Samac for his height. During those years, the Church, the sugar mill, and the *beneficio*, the coffee processing plant, were completed.

In 1970, the main house of the Helmerich family stood empty.

In 1971, 250 Q'eqchi's took possession of the land and organized the Samac Cooperative with an area of 2,250 hectares (5,560 acres). And in 1972, President Carlos Arana Osorio granted title to the land to the Cooperative. The 1973 census lists 417 inhabitants: 202 men and 215 women, 13 of them literate.

Chapter 18

SUSANA LÓPEZ

Tactic, Alta Verapaz
Poqomchi'

I am happy because a woman has to have worth and be recognized," says Susana López, sixty. And she has built a life on that belief.

As a child in the aldea of Tampój, Susana went to school through second grade and learned to weave. Then her parents arranged a marriage for her. She felt as if they were simply giving her away, and that she would go from being their property to becoming someone else's. She went to her godmother, who sent her to their priest. He knew of some nuns in Guatemala City who had a school where she could live, work, and be paid Q. 15 ($2)/month. That became Susana's new home. Among other benefits, the nuns encouraged her to continue her schooling, an opportunity she was glad to take advantage of. At eighteen, having completed fourth grade, Susana returned to Tactic. (Tactic is the municipio and market town of Tampój.)

Susana had two brothers. One was killed by the guerrillas; the other still lives in Tampój, on the land he inherited from their parents. Because girls "had no value or rights," her parents had no reason to leave any land to Susana. So with the money she had saved working at the school, she bought her own piece of land. (In those days, a piece of land 25 by 25 meters (27 by 27 yards) cost Q. 18 ($2.34); Susana bought four pieces.) On this land near the aldea of Chamaoj she grew coffee, avocados, and various kinds of fruit trees. Eventually, Susana did marry, and she and her husband built a small, somewhat fragile house. As her husband worked the land, Susana took up weaving again. They had lived there two years when the 1976 earthquake damaged their house, at which point they bought a lot in the town of Tactic and built a sturdier house there.

In Tactic, there are two traditional huipils. One is lightweight, open and lacy, woven in *calado* (leno). The second is heavier, warmer, and woven with brocaded figures filling all vis-ible space. Tactic is in a cloud forest, meaning that the trees get their moisture from the clouds that often surround them; in terms of flora and fauna, it's like a high-altitude jungle. Because it is so wet, both heat and cold feel more extreme than a thermometer would suggest. Having a lightweight huipil for steamy days and a warmer one for bone-chilling days makes good sense. Some huipils combine the two: a few inches of calado are followed and stabilized by a couple of inches of brocade.

Calado is a technique whose clever structure creates a lacey effect. Warp threads, just a few of them, are twisted around each other, and the weft is put in the space in the middle of the twist. Those twists prevent the plain-weave wefts that come before and after from packing in closely. The result is two rows of open lacey spaces.

When a weaver is creating small amounts of calado, she uses her fingers to make each twist. Weaving an entire cloth of it requires a more efficient method. On a backstrap loom, calado is achieved with the use of extra heddle sticks. The special system of looping a string around the heddle sticks and then around the warp threads creates the twisting all the way across the cloth. Calado is relatively fast to weave; a huipil can be completed in three to eight days. Brocade is slow, with only one row of figures completed in a day; it takes months to complete one huipil. Susana could earn more money weaving and selling less expensive calado huipils than she could weaving and selling fewer higher-priced brocaded huipils. (According to Susana, today a well-woven calado huipil sells for Q. 75 ($9.75) to 100 ($13), a brocaded huipil Q. 2,500 ($325) to 3,000 ($390).

And Susana's earnings became increasingly important. Along with working her land and weaving, Susana and her husband began a family. However, the marriage was not good. When Susana had one daughter and four sons, the marriage ended. Susana's mother and grandmother encouraged her to stay, but once again,

Susana López's beauty reflects the presence she carries within. This huipil is lightweight for when the cloud forest is warm and muggy. While she does have necklaces with special meanings, this one, made of silver coins, has no special significance besides being stunning.

as confirmation of herself as a valuable and capable woman, Susana took on the responsibility of raising her five children on her own. By weaving.

"It takes concentration to weave. I would close my door to avoid being bothered by people going by, and I would weave all day. I sold in the local market because when the children were small, I couldn't leave."

Susana knew that getting a good education was essential for her children. She still worked on her land herself, and she would walk around saying, "These avocados mean notebooks, this *mispero* (a fruit) is paper and pencils." After keeping her children healthy, her children's education was the focus of her life.

Over the years, Susana wove, worked her land, buying more land when she could. For a few years, she worked in rural communities as a health promoter and with literacy programs. When the market for weaving dropped off, she put more attention into working the land—always in traje. "I would come home from the fields with pounds of mud around the hem of my corte. I loved it, but it was hard work." Finally, from the strain of years of intense weaving and agricultural work, she began to have significant back pain. Her vision was also going. It was time for a new activity.

Susana's years of effort toward her children's education have paid off. All have graduated and are working in professional jobs. She still lives in the house they all grew up in, now considerably more elegant and comfortable than it was in those struggling years. Her children, observing her physical pains and the shift in the financial situation of the whole family have suggested the obvious: "Mom, why don't you take a break? You can do that now."

It is not in Susana's nature to take a break. She can't weave, but she does still want to have textiles in her hands. She likes having her own money, and she likes getting out to see people. So now she sells other people's huipils, rebozos, and other textiles. Her two best markets are four hours away in Guatemala City: *Museo Ixchel del Traje Indigena* and the *Mercado de Artesania* (Ixchel Museum of Indigenous Dress and the Artisan Market). Two of her children live in the city, so the trips have a double benefit.

Living with Susana are her thirteen-year-old granddaughter, Flor de María, who prefers small Tactic to huge Guatemala City where her parents live, and her eighty-year-old mother, María.

María still loves to weave and does so every day. Whereas Susana doesn't like weaving all-white pieces because they're bor-

Opposite left: These two huipils were woven differently but both are warm for when the cloud forest turns chilly and damp. Of the traje shown in this book, only the huipils from Alta Verapaz are not tucked into their cortes. Here the corte has a drawstring so the eight varas of fabric are all gathered around the waist. The huipil, light or heavy, hangs freely outside, giving an entirely different look.

Center: Having land for agriculture was one of the most critical elements in Susana's ability to raise her five children. She still owns the original plots she bought when she was sixteen years old.

Susana's mother María, eighty, divides her time between living with Susana or her brother, who lives on the land where they grew up. María still weaves every day, without glasses.

ing—color is where the excitement is—María doesn't like to weave white because it gets dirty too easily. María gets tired now, so she does not weave as much; however, she still loves it and she is still selling, so she is still weaving.

María's younger sister Modesta has always been a "sales rep" for both María and Susana, traveling around the country as well as to Guatemala City from her home in Tampój. But at seventy-five, Modesta has slowed down some, too. Her primary sales location now is in *Parque Central*, Central Park in Guatemala City. Between the National Palace, the National Cathedral, and many special events in the park, there is plenty of traffic, both tourist and Guatemalan, to enjoy and buy beautiful textiles from Alta Verapaz. Modesta also has a daughter living in the city, so as with Susana, she benefits doubly in being there.

When we were talking with Flor de María, we asked her if she spoke Poqomchi'. As is often the case with the younger generation, she said no. She understands it some but does not speak it. At the possibility of her learning it, Susana chimed in. "No, better Q'eqchi'. Very few people speak Poqomchi'." It's a bridge language between Q'eqchi' and Poqom. According to Susana, if a Q'eqchi speaker were hungry in a Poqom village, he could starve to death, the two languages are so different. (Q'eqchi' is the third largest linguistic group in Guatemala.)

We asked Susana if she had anything to say to the people reading her story.

"When I was a little girl, one day someone passing me on the street said, 'Oh, how poor!' I wanted to understand what that meant, so I went to stores to see what people who did not look poor looked like. Their hair was clean and combed, and their clothes were clean and cared for. They looked like they valued themselves. I began to do the same." As we were about to leave, Susana showed us a tablecloth she would be selling to Museo Ixchel. It was nine *lienzos* (panels) of pijbil white on white that she had bought from weavers she works with and then crocheted together, also with white. It was beautiful.

"A woman needs to value herself in every way," Susana says. "Work is beautiful. Someone who sits around not doing anything is not valuing herself. No matter what work a woman does, she needs to value herself enough to do it well."

Chapter 19

CATARINA AMPEREZ SIANA
San Rafael, Rabinal, Baja Verapaz
Achi

D*oña* Catarina has outlived two husbands. So far. When I stopped by before our photo-taking visit to be sure she would be available, I asked if she would be home, not out with her boyfriend. "Bring me one!" she laughed, almost jumping off her little bench.

Born in 1930 in Chicpajoj, Catarina was eight years old when she learned to spin from her mother. She was the chip, the youngest in her family, and the only one to learn to spin. As she was growing up, her mother also taught her the other skills girls needed to learn, including weaving, cooking, grinding corn, and making tortillas.

Now eighty-four and struggling with high blood pressure, gastritis, and Parkinson's Disease, Catarina has done a lot of living since then. Always sitting on her favorite little bench—she is a tiny woman—she told us stories.

When she was fifteen, her parents arranged her marriage. She and her husband lived in Guachiplin, but were gone half of every year to work on the coast. "It was different then. There were no roads, no electricity, no cars, no airplanes. Now there are lots of airplanes! Of course, there weren't many people, either." So without roads or cars they walked to the coast, to Escuintla. Most of the time they worked in the sugar fields, sometimes they served meals to the other workers, and part of the time they worked in the cotton fields "cleaning cotton." Did she ever harvest coffee? "No! Too muddy, too many flies, too many mosquitoes. Awful!" They were there from November to April every year, returning when it was time to plant the corn.

Catarina loved to spin and weave. She said that as a child learning she was silly and inattentive and her mother would scold her, telling her she was deaf! But somehow the lessons sank in and now in response to the question, "Did you like to weave?" she smiles broadly. "Oh, yes. I wove when I was a girl and kept weaving my whole life." Her health problems keep her from weaving now, but weaving was clearly a happy part of her life.

She and her husband had two children, a boy and a girl. When her children were small, Catarina's husband fell from an orange tree and was killed instantly. "Just for some oranges," she lamented. That was October 1. In November, she went back to the coast with her two children, as always. At the age of five, her daughter died while they were at the coast.

When Catarina was in the Rabinal area, she spun cotton and wove textiles for herself and her family, and additional pieces to sell. No one wanted to pay the price for something totally handspun, so she used commercial yarn for the warp and her handspun for the weft. She sold servilletas, tablecloths, bedding, and whatever else would sell. She went to the market in Rabinal to sell on Sundays, and again said, "It wasn't like it is now. Now, they have booths to sell from. Then, we just sat on the ground with a basket in front of us."

Catarina met her second husband in Rabinal, and when they married, she moved to San Rafael. They had five children, of whom three are still alive. Her husband died seven years ago after more than fifty years together, and Catarina still lives where they did most of those years.

As she sold in the market, he worked as a day laborer. They worked hard and saved every cent they could, and finally were able to buy a piece of land. Thinking back to that time, her whole body winced and she started to tear up. "It was so hard then, we were so poor."

But their land had enough space for their cornfield—and for cotton. They brought seeds home from the coast and planted enough to supply all the cotton she needed. With each harvest, she saved seeds and used them to plant her next crop.

She showed us her beautiful old dark brown spindle with its

Catarina still has the touch that turns clouds into thread.

Below: While the paint job has changed over the years, the supported spindle is still made with a low-fire ceramic whorl.

Opposite: Catarina in her San Rafael traje: brocaded huipil, red bead necklace, and a tocoyal like the one she received on her wedding day. Not the traditional Rabinal style, her corte comes from Salcajá, as do most in the Rabinal area, because they are so much cooler in the brutally hot climate.

broken whorl, the clay ball near the bottom. "I can't spin much anymore. See this old broken spindle? And how worn down the bottom tip is? You can't get these anymore." She knows that spinning has nearly vanished in her area, but wasn't aware that it is still going on in a few places in the country.

As we talked about how she gets from plant to yarn, Catarina surprised us. Because she grew her own cotton, she could work with the bolls one by one. As she picked the bolls open and apart, she would also pull out the seeds and keep picking the fibers apart, the only "carding" she did. Other spinners in Guatemala lay their cotton fiber out on a *petate* (a reed mat). They then use two forked sticks to slap or beat the fibers until they're separated enough to make spinning easier. Catarina knows about that method, but she always worked in her lap, picking, picking, with her fingers only. When the fibers were separated enough, she would start to spin. It is clear watching her that Catarina's hands still have the skills developed and perfected over more than seventy-five years. In spite of the Parkinson's, her hands work well.

Catarina has not been able to convince her daughter, daughters-in-law, or granddaughters to take up spinning. Some of them, as well as her sons, can spin but don't. "*Cuesta!* (It's hard!)" Her daughter and daughters-in-law weave on backstrap looms, some pieces to sell as well as for their families. But her granddaughters are going to school—one even studied in Iowa for two years as part of a cultural exchange program. Although they may know how to spin and weave, it's unlikely that either will be a big part of their lives.

Catarina lives with one of her sons and his family, and all her other children take turns bringing her food, so there is always a lot of family around.

Our visit was a grand event. When we arrived to take pictures, we found out that Catarina had just returned from her daughter's house, where she had gone to use the temascal (Mayan sauna) in preparation for her big afternoon. Though the path to her house is quite rugged, we did not really appreciate the enormity of that until we saw her move from a chair to her little bench. Over the course of our many visits, she had always welcomed us from the little bench where she spends her days. This time when we arrived, she was sitting in a plastic chair with arms. It would have been comfortable except that Catarina is so small that in a chair designed for normal-sized people, her feet stuck straight out in front of her. We had her move to her little bench, and for the first time saw her standing up. As she took four steps from chair to bench, even with help, she looked like her body was made of jello. Trying to imagine her traversing that path, that even for us took some skill, was beyond imagining. It showed how important this visit was to her.

We got the same message when we talked about traditional and fiesta clothing, including the tocoyal that is Rabinal's special head adornment. "Do you want to see me dressed in mine?" Of course we did! So Catarina and a contingency of granddaughters went inside the house while we waited, visiting with three generations of family members. After quite awhile, she emerged, dressed in her finest. Although her corte and huipil were gorgeous, her tocoyal demanded the most attention.

The two colorful tube-shaped pieces above her forehead are made the same way a pom-pom is made, of which there are many in Guatemala. But these are long instead of round, and are stiff and hard rather than soft. They do not curve with the shape of a head. On a woman as small as Catarina, they practically hide the rest of her head, and it seemed as if they would fall off at any minute. They never did. The tocoyal is given to a woman on her wedding day, so traditionally anyone wearing one was known to be married. In the past, most women wore them all the time, and

some older women still say that they feel half-dressed if they go to town without their tocoyal. More common, however, is wearing them only for special occasions, such as Semana Santa.

We could tell that Catarina was very tired, so we packed up to go. Although we had worn her out completely, as we were leaving, Catarina waved her hand across the whole space full of family members playing together and said, "Thank you, for all of this happiness."

A happy Catarina sits forward in her chair, surrounded by some of her fifty-plus offspring.

COTTON—
FROM PEASANT TO KING TO PEASANT

The story of cotton in Guatemala goes back to the time before time, when Hunahpú, second King of the K'iche's, was surprised to discover the silky fibers of the cotton plant. As he idly twisted them around his fingers, creating thread that seemed like the hair of monkeys and men, he had visions of ways it could be used, a dreaming that led not only to thread but also to dyes, looms, clothing, and an eternal connection to nature.

More recently, from only 7,500 years ago (5500 BC), archaeologists and paleobotanists have found evidence of cotton as a domesticated plant harvested by the Maya in Mexico and Guatemala. For long stretches of time, cotton was used in all its forms (raw, spun, and woven) to pay taxes, as special gifts, for clothing used in ceremonies and rituals, and even as armor for warriors. Small bits of cotton cloth were used as coins, and in general cotton was as valuable as cacao and *quetzal* feathers. Ropes and hammocks are obvious uses; less common were sacrifices to the gods and medicinal uses. All of this was before the Spanish ever set foot in the New World.

By the 1970s cotton had become one of the most important crops in Guatemala, with 125,000 hectares (over 308,800 acres) of land producing 362.5 million pounds of cotton in 1979. Fewer than twenty-five years later it was gone from Guatemala, a victim of global economics.

But one farm survived, albeit reduced in size, and now the fourth generation of the Villavicencio family has shifted focus and is the sole grower of natural-colored cotton. Historically native to Guatemala, in addition to creamy white, cotton can be grown in brown, green, gray, rose, and variations of those colors.

Brown cotton, called *ixcaco* or *cuyuscate*, is the best known and can be found in many older textiles, especially those woven prior to the ascendance of commercially spun yarn. A soft cocoa color, handspun ixcaco enriches a huipil in a way no other yarn can.

Other than for their own use, the cotton from the Villavicencio farm is sold only to Proteje, a project of Museo Ixchel. Proteje's mission is the resurrection of traditional materials and techniques used to create Guatemalan textiles in millennia past, and naturally colored cotton is an important part of that tradition.

Chapter 20

Ana María Gonzalez Cirin (Daughter of Cecilia Cirin)

Guatemala City
Kaqchikel

Living in two cultures at the same time can be hard. There are many reasons people do it, with economics and safety probably at the top of the list. In Ana María Gonzalez Cirin's case, it's economics.

Ana Maria, thirty-six, was born in Saquitacaj, an aldea 3 kilometers (1.9 miles) from its municipio, San José Poaquil. When she was two, she went to live with her grandmother, and from her learned the skills girls learn as they grow up, including weaving. Ana loved to weave and learned all the varied techniques in the Poaquil huipil (see page 12). Later in her life, she would use that same mix of techniques and yarns to weave highly unconventional huipils, such as one with a large tiger crossing the entire front of the body. But, then, Ana was unconventional from the beginning.

At fourteen, Ana moved to Guatemala City, where she lived with a family as an all-around helper. It was a good family, and Ana was able to keep weaving. When she had her son, Manuel, the mother of the family advised Ana to not marry the father, whom she believed to be less than reliable. Her predictions proved true, and Ana chose to pursue life as the single mother of a son who is the light of her life.

Living with that family continued to be good, in part because of the blessing of Manuel being welcome also. But a job as a domestic rarely lasts forever, and eventually the children of that family grew up and moved away. The mother told Ana she was welcome to stay, but she could no longer pay her a salary. Knowing she would need money to support Manuel, Ana thanked the woman but did not stay.

Then twenty-four, Ana went back to Poaquil and her grandmother's house, and for a beautiful ten months, she was able to enjoy her son and weave to her heart's content. During that time she also began to understand what would be required of her for raising Manuel and for her own future return to Poaquil. Ana knew that she needed a salary and that the only place she could get it was in the city. With a second-grade education her options were limited, and being a domestic was better than working in a factory. So she went back.

Since then, Ana has had a number of jobs, each with its own personality. She has learned many things about city life that were not part of Poaquil life: ironing, cooking a different kind of food, and speaking better Spanish, to name a few. The family finds it amusing that now her sisters call Ana to ask advice on how to do some of those things. She is happy to tell them, and she adds, with a smile, "But don't ask me for advice about your husbands. I've never been married so I don't know."

For Ana, everything is about Manuel. The jobs she has had since she returned to the city haven't allowed Manuel to be with her. When she first left Poaquil, he lived half-time with her grandmother and half-time with her mother. Since her grandmother died in 2007, he has lived with Ana's mother full-time. In most of Ana's jobs, she has had weekends off, giving her what she most desperately wants—time to spend with her son. He is thirteen now, and Ana aches for having missed his childhood. Aches, and accepts that that was the price she paid for the benefits. Manuel is in school, loves it, and will continue. He is healthy and happy, part of an extended family, and living a good life in Saquitacaj.

In addition to supporting Manuel, Ana is investing in her own future back in Saquitacaj. Without her grandmother, she has no reason to return to Poaquil. So Ana is investing in land and building a house a short distance from her mother and sisters. When Ana was growing up, she called her grandmother Mom and her mother by her name, Cecilia. "Having my own son," she says, "taught me how my mother feels, how much she loves me. Now I call her Mom."

Ana likes the family she works for now; they are good people. She is sorry that she gets to go home only every other weekend, but she makes the most of it when she does. Enjoying Manuel, weaving with her sisters, spending time with her mother, and being on the land that will be her home … all these feed her soul.

It is Ana's plan to keep working for as long as Manuel continues in school. Once he graduates, she wants to leave the city, which has had its advantages but is not home. She will return to life in the aldea, where she will be with her family and have time to weave.

Ana does her best in a world that is not her own until she can go home again.

Epilogue

Although most of the artisans you have met in this book come from small communities in rural areas, there is reason to include someone in Guatemala City as well. As you have seen, many of the artisans have children living away, in vastly different cultures. Being able to first introduce Cecilia Cirin, who misses her daughter, and end with her daughter Ana, who misses her family and longs for the day she can go home, tells the story from both sides.

And that, to us, is one of the gifts we have received in researching and writing this book: getting to know the story from more sides, theirs and ours, inside and outside. In the conversations we have had with the artisans, and between ourselves in reviewing what we learned, and in telling other people about our experiences, we have been silenced more than once, felt much, ached deeply, cried hard, and laughed even harder. We have been confused, humbled, and awed.

As stated at the outset, our main objective was to speak with artisans about their lives, as artisans and as people. As unobtrusively as possible we asked questions such as, Did you ever not weave? Could you spin on the coast or only at home? Do you make baskets because you love to make baskets or because you have to? Do you do all the steps of the process yourself? Can your life and your art be separated? The answer to the last question is no. As for selling, it is so much a part of the picture that it cannot be separated either. These artisans love to weave, love to sell, and love to teach, to pass their skills on. It's all part of the story.

The people we came to know have been through many tough times, some more severe than most of us can imagine. And still they are so filled with spirit, with hope, determination, pride, and even joy, that it inspires those things in us. Looking at this gift from their side, in the end they all said the same thing: "Thank you for coming and listening. I am grateful to be acknowledged, to have my value recognized."

GLOSSARY

A

Abuela – grandmother

Abuelo – grandfather

Achiote – a plant whose seeds yield a red substance used as a condiment and for dyeing

Acordonado – old-style wool blanket, plaid 2/2 twill

Alguacil – sheriff

Alcalde – mayor

Aldea – village

Amarrador/a – one who ties jaspe knots

Añil – a name for indigo

Atol – hot corn-based drink

Ayotc – kind of squash

B

Batanando – fulling wool blankets in hot water

Bejuco – a kind of vine

Beneficio – place where coffee is processed from cherry to ready-for-roasting

Bordado – embroidered

Brocado – brocade, supplementary weft weaving techniques

C

Calado – leno, a lacey weave formed by twisting warp threads

Chilacayote – squash used to make candy and beverages; it resembles a watermelon

Chuchitos – corn masa with meat and salsa inside

Cinta – hair ribbons or wraps

Cochineal – an insect that lives on cactus; it yields a red dye

Cofrade – member of the cofradía

Cofradía – brotherhood originally formed as a bridge between the Catholic Church and Maya practices

Comal – slightly curved griddle for making tortillas

Comerciante – business person

Conflicto Armado – Armed Conflict, Time of Violence

Copal – type of incense used in Maya ceremonies

Cordel – group of threads tied together for dyeing one part of a jaspe design

Corte – traditional skirt

Costal – large bag woven of strips of a combination of polyethylene and polypropylene, used for grain and much more

Coton or chaqueta – traditional men's ceremonial jacket

Crea – red yarn used to make the creya

Creya – red band across the shoulders of Comalapa huipils

D

Departamento – department, equivalent to a state in the United States or a province in Canada

Don, Doña – title of respect (we chose to use it for the artisans who are more than eighty years old)

E

Elote – corn on the cob

Encomiendas – system of forced labor and heavy taxes imposed by the Spanish

F

Faja – belt

Feria Titular – annual fair every town has to honor its patron saint

Finca – large farm or plantation

G

Güicoy – small round vegetable that can be substituted for zucchini

Güisquil – dark green pear-shaped watery vegetable good in soups or on its own

H

Huipil – woman's traditional upper garment

I

Indigo – plant used to make a blue dye; Levis were originally dyed with indigo. Also called añil or jiquilite

J

Jabón de coche – soap made with pork lard

Jaspe – sophisticated tie-dye technique performed on yarn before it's woven

Jiquilite – a species of indigo
Jornalero – day worker
Judiciales – the most vicious of the police during the Conflicto Armado

K

Kanac – traditional food resembling a tamalito
K'ot – two-headed eagle

L

Ladino/a – anyone who is not Maya
Lienzo – strip or panel of cloth

M

Maguey – also known as agave, sisal, and henequén, a plant with large spikey leaves from which is extracted a stiff fiber used for ropes and cords of varying thicknesses.
Malacate – clay ball at the bottom of a spindle
Manchado – space-dyed yarns (usually means spotted or stained)
Manta – cloth-like flour-sacking; muslin
Masa – corn after it has been ground (wet)
Mecapal – tumpline, forehead strap for carrying things on one's back
Mechas – pre-cut pieces for tying knotted rugs
Milpa – cornfield
Mimbre – wicker
Mish – once a specific brand of cotton thread; now used for any mercerized cotton
Mispero – very sweet yellow fruit the size of a plum
Morral – shoulder bag

Municipio – municipality; similar to a county in the United States

O

Olla – pot or pan

P

Pacaya – a palm that provides both food and decorative material
Pantalón – traditional men's pants
Patrón – an owner or boss, one who hires someone
Peinando – brushing wool blankets to make them fluffy
People of the Corn – the Maya
Perraje – shawl
Petate – reed mat
Piedra de moler – grinding stone, volcanic
Pita – small rope, sisal in the past but now synthetic as well
Pom – kind of incense for ceremonial fires
Poncho – garment or blanket
Popol Vuh – sacred book of the K'iche' that includes the history of their people

Q

Quetzal (bird) – national bird of Guatemala, most notable for its 63.5-centimeter (25-inch) long tail that flows out behind it when it flies
Quetzal (money) – currency of Guatemala; it has the same coin denominations as the U.S. dollar; abbreviated Q.

R

Ralo, raja – loose, open

Randa – embroidered seam covering
Rebozo – shawl
Regidor – assistant to the assistant mayor
Remesas – money sent to families in Guatemala from people in the United States, Canada, and other countries
Ruedina – spindle-style spinning wheel made with a bicycle wheel

S

Sedalina – DMC perle cotton embroidery thread
Semana Santa – Holy Week, between Palm Sunday and Easter
Servilleta – small all-purpose cloth
Sobrehuipil – ceremonial huipil woven full length and wider to go over the daily huipil and corte

T

Tamal – soft corn masa, usually with meat and salsa inside
Tamalito – firmer corn masa, only masa, eaten in some places instead of tortillas
Tejidos – weavings, cloths
-tenango – place of
Tiempo de la Violencia – Time of the Violence
Tienda – store
Tinaja – narrow-necked jug for carrying water
Tocoyal – head adornment
Torno – spindle-style spinning wheel with solid wood drive wheel
Traje – traditional clothing
Triangulo Ixil – Ixil Triangle, made up of Chajul, Cotzal, and Nebaj
Tributos – tributes, taxes
Tupido – tighter

Tupuy – hair adornment of Cobán
Tzute – large all-purpose cloth, also a
    ceremonial cloth

V

Vara – measurement equal to 84 cm
    (33.6 inches)

W

Warp – threads attached to a loom,
    lengthwise in the final fabric
Weft – threads woven cross-wise into the
    warp, woven selvedge to selvedge

BIBLIOGRAPHY

Note: Museo Ixchel has published books under at least three different names. We have used Museo Ixchel for all of them.

Anderson, Marilyn. *Artes y Artesanas de Mayas de Guatemala.* Rochester, New York: Yatut Ix Balin, 2009.
—*Granddaughters of Corn.* Willimantic, Connecticut: Curbstone Press, 1988.
—*Guatemalan Textiles Today.* New York: Watson-Guptill, 1978.

Asturias de Barrios, Linda, and Barbara Knoke de Arathoon. *Cuyuscate: Brown Cotton in the Textile Tradition of Guatemala.* Guatemala City, Guatemala: Museo Ixchel, 2002.

Asturias de Barrios, Linda, Comalapa: *Native Dress and its Significance.* Guatemala City, Guatemala: Museo Ixchel, 1985.

Atwater, Mary M. *Guatemala Visited.* Shuttle Craft Guild, 1946 and 1965.

Barber, Elizabeth W. *Women's Work: The First 20,000 Years.* New York: W. W. Norton & Company, 1994.

Bertrand, Regis, and Danielle Magna. *The Textiles of Guatemala.* London, England: Studio Editions Limited, 1991.

Chandler, Deborah, and Raymond Senuk. *Guatemalan Woven Wealth: Preserving a Rich Textile Tradition.* Friendship Bridge, 2009.

Dieterich, Mary , Jon T. Erickson, and Erin Younger. *Heard Museum: Guatemalan Costumes—The Heard Museum Collection.* 1979.

Emery, Irene. *The Primary Structure of Fabrics.* Washington, D.C.: The Textile Museum, 1966.
Gaitán, Hector. *Los Presidentes de Guatemala.* Guatemala City, Guatemala: Ediciones Artemis-Edinter, 1992.

Girard de Marroquín, Anne. *Rostros de la Guatemala Indígena.* Guatemala City, Guatemala: Museo Ixchel 2012.

Guatemalan Textiles—2008 Trunk Show, and Benefit Sale, Friendship Bridge, 2008.

Hecht, Ann. *Textiles from Guatemala.* Seattle, Washington: University of Washington Press, 2001.

Hempstead, William, ed. *Maya Huipiles of Guatemala* (a map). Guatemala City, Guatemala: Museo Ixchel, 2011.

Hendrickson, Carol. *Weaving Identities—Construction of Dress and Self in a Highland Guatemala Town.* Austin, Texas: University of Texas Press, 1995.

Holsbeke, Mireille, and Julia Montoya. *Tejidos Mayas—El Rostro de las palabras y los pensamientos tejidos.* Catálogo Chiapas y Guatemala Siglos XIX y XX, Etnografisch Museum Antwerpen y Cholsamaj, 2003.

Knoke, Barbara, and Raymond Senuk. *Embroidery—Stitches that Unite Cultures.* Guatemala City, Guatemala: Museo Ixchel 2010.

Kojima, Hideo. *World of Color. Friends of the Ixchel Museum* newsletter, December 2007.

McKenzie, Christopher James. *Religion, Community, and Identity: Perspectives on the Cult of San Simón in Guatemala.* Edmonton, Alberta, Canada: University of Alberta, 1998.

Miralbés de Polanco, Rosario, Eugenia Saénz de Tejada, and Idalma Mejia de Rodas. Zunil—*Costume and Economy, Revised Edition.* Guatemala City, Guatemala: Museo Ixchel, 1990 and 1996.

Morales Hidalgo, Italo. *La Situación de Jaspe en Guatemala.* Sub-Centro Regional de Artesanías y Artes Populares, Colección Tierra Adentro 4, 1984.

Petterson, Carmen. *Maya of Guatemala—Life and Dress.* Guatemala City, Guatemala: Museo Ixchel, 1976.

Quirín Diesseldorff, Dr. Herbert. X Balam *Q'ué, El Pájaro Sol.* Guatemala City, Guatemala: Museo Ixchel, 1984.

Rousso, Kathryn. *Maguey Journey: Discovering Textiles in Guatemala.* Tucson, Arizona: University of Arizona Press, 2010.

Rowe, Anne Pollard. *A Century of Change in Guatemalan Textiles.* Center for Inter-American Relations, 1981.

Shaughnessy, Roxanne, curator. *Ancestry and Artistry—Maya Textiles from Guatemala.* Toronto, Ontario, Canada: Textile Museum of Canada, 2013.

Sperlich, Norbert. and Elizabeth Katz Sperlich. *Guatemalan Backstrap Weaving.* Norman, Oklahoma: University of Oklahoma Press, 1980.

Tidball, Harriet. *A Weaver's Guatemala.* Shuttle Craft Guild, 1966.

Ventura, Carol. *Maya Hair Sashes Backstrap Woven in Jacaltenango, Guatemala.* Self-published, 2003.

Vecchiato, Gianni, and Azzo Ghidinelli. *Guatemala Rainbow.* Portland, Oregon: Pomegranate Artbooks Inc., 1989.

Wilson, Laura. *Stories of Survival, Mayan Elders Share their Memories.* Vermillion, South Dakota: Sharing the Dream in Guatemala, 2009.

www.deguate.com

www.epocacolonialdeguatemala.blogspot.com

SUPPORTIVE ORGANIZATIONS

The following organizations work to support Guatemalan weavers and traditional weaving.

Museo Ixchel de Traje Indigena – Ixchel Museum of Indigenous Dress
www.museoixchel.org

Proteje – natural-colored cotton project of the museum
www.textilesproteje.com
6 Calle final, Zona 10
Centro Cultural UFM (University Francisco Marroquin)
Guatemala City, Guatemala
011 (502) 2361-8081, -8082, -8084

Casa del Tejido Antiguo
– House of Antique Textiles (Museum)
www.museodeltejido.org
www.laantigua-guatemala.com/Museo-Tienda_Casa
_del_Tejido.htm
1 Calle Poniente, Número 51
La Antigua Guatemala, Guatemala
011 (502) 7832-3169

Aj Quen – fair trade and education
www.ajquen.com
Km. 56 Carretera Panamericana
Chimaltenango, Guatemala
011 (502) 7839-1725, -4126

Cojolya Asociación de Tejedoras Mayas
– fair trade and museum
www.cojolya.org
Cojolya Association
8256 NW 30th Terrace
Doral, FL 33122

Comercial las Máscaras 2nd nivel
Calle Real, Cantón Tzunjuyá
Santiago Atitlán, Sololá, Guatemala
011 (502) 7721-7268

Cultural Cloth
– Provides markets and other support, founder of
Multicolores—rug-hooking project
www.culturalcloth.com
W. 3560 State Hwy. 35
The Great River Road
Maiden Rock, WI 54750
(715) 607-1238

Calle Peatonal Capulín, Zona 2
Panajachel, Sololá, Guatemala
011 (502) 7762-2226
multicolores.org

ClothRoads
– online marketplace, artisan story-telling, documentation,
and economic support
www.clothroads.com
306 N. Washington, Suite 104
Loveland, CO 80537
(970) 685-4964

Maya Traditions Foundation
– education, health, and fair trade
Fundación Tradiciones Mayas
www.mayatraditions.org
Casa del Arbol
Callejon Chotzar
Panajachel, Sololá, Guatemala
011 (502) 7762-2829

Maya Works – fair trade, education, and micro-credit
www.mayaworks.org
1937 Maple Avenue
Berwyn, IL 60402
(312) 243-8050

6 Calle 4-70, Zona 1
Quinta los Aposentos
Chimaltenango, Guatemala
011 (502) 7839-5853

Mayan Hands – fair trade and education
www.mayanhands.org
92 Brookline
Albany, NY 12203
(518) 438-5636

Asociación Tejedoras Unidas (Komon Ajkem)
2 Avenida 02-13, Zona 18
Guatemala City, Guatemala
011 (502) 2260-7295

Friends of Sharing the Dream in Guatemala
– fair trade and more
www.sharingthedream.org
10 West Main Street
Vermillion, SD 57069
(605) 624-6895

Asociación Compartiendo Sueños
1a. Avenida 1-64, zona 3, Calle Salpores
Tel: 011 (502) 7762-0099
Panajachel, Sololá, Guatemala

Y´abal Handicrafts – fair trade
www.yabal-handicrafts.com
12 Avenida 3-35, Zona l
Quetzaltenango, Guatemala
011 (502) 7761-7760

Friendship Bridge – micro-credit and education
www.friendshipbridge.org
405 Urban Street, Suite 140
Lakewood CO 80228
(303) 674-0717

Avenida Santander 5-38, Zona 2
Panajachel, Sololá, Guatemala
011 (502) 7762-0222

WARP - Weave A Real Peace
– networking organization for textile-based development work
www.weavearealpeace.org
3102 N. Classen Boulevard, PMB 249
Oklahoma City, OK 73118

INDEX

MORE BOOKS FROM THRUMS

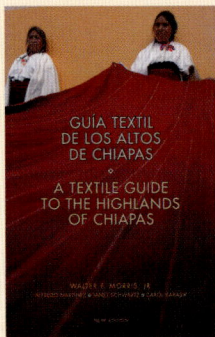

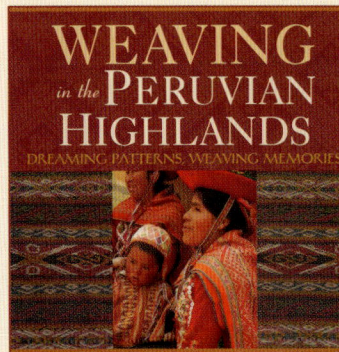

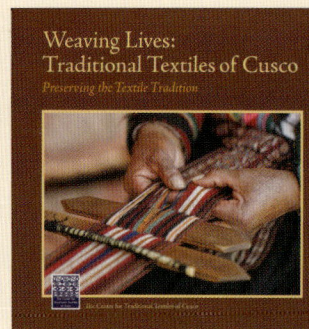

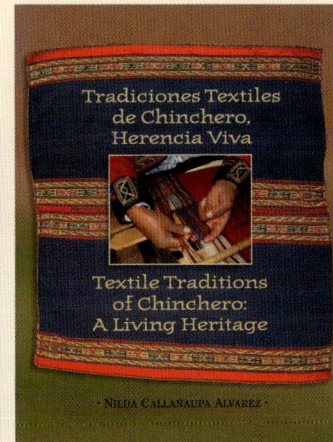

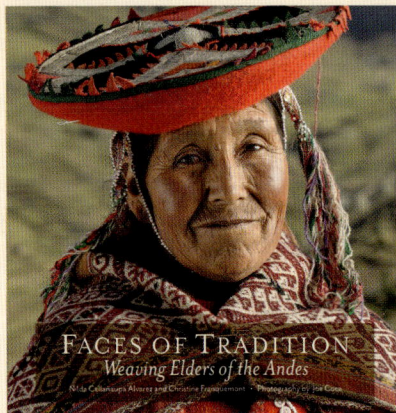

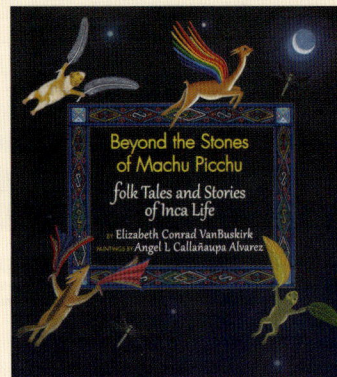

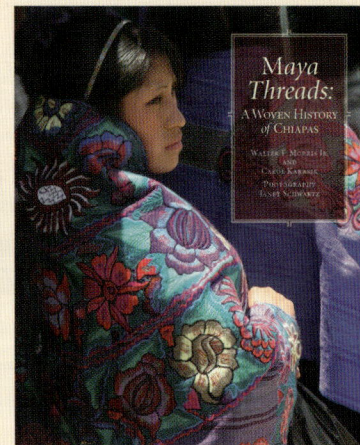

GUÍA TEXTIL
DE LOS ALTOS
DE CHIAPAS
•
A TEXTILE GUIDE
TO THE HIGHLANDS
OF CHIAPAS

WEAVING
in the
PERUVIAN
HIGHLANDS
DREAMING PATTERNS, WEAVING MEMORIES

Weaving Lives:
Traditional Textiles of Cusco
Preserving the Textile Tradition

Tradiciones Textiles
de Chinchero,
Herencia Viva

Textile Traditions
of Chinchero:
A Living Heritage

NILDA CALLAÑAUPA ALVAREZ

FACES OF TRADITION
Weaving Elders of the Andes

Beyond the Stones
of Machu Picchu
Folk Tales and Stories
of Inca Life
by Elizabeth Conrad VanBuskirk
paintings by Angel L. Callañaupa Alvarez

Maya
Threads:
A Woven History
of Chiapas